The
Problem Solving
Memory
Jogger™

Seven Steps to
Improved Processes

First Edition

GOAL/QPC

The Problem Solving Memory Jogger™
Seven Steps to Improved Processes

Development Team

Writers
Michael Brassard
Carolyn Field
Fran Oddo
Bob Page
Diane Ritter
Larry Smith

Copy Editors
Fran Oddo
Dan Picard

Cover and Book Design
Michele Kierstead

Graphics Production
Carolyn Field
Michele Kierstead
Fran Oddo
Dan Picard

GOAL/QPC

12B Manor Parkway, Salem, NH 03079-2862

Toll free: 800-643-4316   **Phone:** 603-893-1944
Fax: 603-870-9122 **E-mail:**service@goalqpc.com
Web site: www.goalqpc.com

Printed in the United States of America
First Edition
10 9 8 7 6 5
ISBN 1-57681-031-3

Acknowledgments

We extend our sincere thanks to the following people for their insights, suggestions, and encouragement throughout the development of this book.

Concept and Content Reviewers

Linda Antonie
American Airlines

Charles F. Boudreau
Quality Dimensions, Inc.

Doug Daetz
Hewlett-Packard Co.

Pamela Dunham
GE Aircraft Engines

Alan H. Field
MicroTouch Systems, Inc.

Nicolas P. Governale
Governale & Associates

Leigh Anne Griffin
PacifiCare

Lorin House
PacifiCare

Francis Kim
Medtronic, Inc.

Peggy McGibney
First Data Merchant Services

Weston Milliken
CUE Consulting

Linda Phillips
Honeywell Electronic Materials

Sumathi Ravindra Raj
Global Quality & Engineering Consulting

Aleta Richards
Buyer Corporation

Lynne Rosiak
PacifiCare

Larry Smith
Ford Motor Company

Luby Weaver
North Carolina Community College System

John B. Wright
Lifetime Learning, Inc.

How to Use
The Problem Solving Memory Jogger™

The Problem Solving Memory Jogger™ is designed for you to use on the job or in the classroom. This book uses a **problem-solving model** based upon a variety of data and knowledge-based tools. The emphasis of this model is on **root cause analysis** and **innovative solutions**.

Use this book as part of a **self-study** program or as a reference before, during, and after **training** to learn the concepts, methods, and basic tools for effective problem solving. Each step in *The Problem Solving Memory Jogger™* details the key concepts and the practical skills that you should master. The book also highlights a **case example** that demonstrates how the tools are used in each step in the process.

You'll also find page references to supporting books that include step-by-step details on tool construction and the team process. The shorthand references in this text are:

Reference	Shorthand
The Creativity Tools Memory Jogger™	CTMJ
The Memory Jogger™ II	MJII
The Memory Jogger™ 9000/2000	MJ9000/2000
The Project Management Memory Jogger™	PMMJ
The Team Memory Jogger™	TMJ

You can also find the information in electronic form on the CD-ROM *The Memory Jogger™ E-Book Series*. It provides the full text for the tools and topics from five of GOAL/QPC's most popular pocket guides (listed above).

What do the different icons mean?

 Getting Ready–When you see this runner, expect a brief description of the purpose of a step *(What does this step do?)*, along with the necessary concepts and actions you'll need to be effective in implementing the steps of the problem-solving model. *(What concepts must I understand to do this step?* and *What actions must be taken in this step?)*

 Cruising–When you see this runner, expect to find step-by-step instructions or guidelines for a step or tool. *(How do I do it?)*

 Finishing the Course–When you see this runner, you are reading the case example that is featured throughout the book.

 Tips–When you see this figure, you'll get tips on a step, tool use, or team behavior.

 Turbo-charging–When you see this icon, you'll get ideas for unique and innovative ways to enhance your team's problem-solving efforts. Get comfortable with the basic steps but when your team is ready, move to a higher level of performance with *How can I turbo-charge this step?*

Snapshot of the 7-Step Model

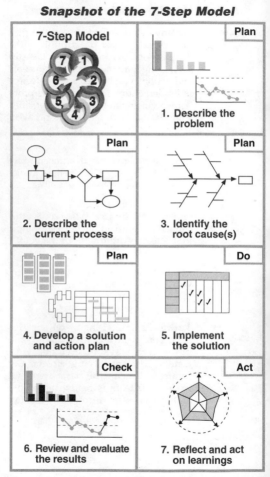

7-Step Model

Plan

1. Describe the problem

Plan

2. Describe the current process

Plan

3. Identify the root cause(s)

Plan

4. Develop a solution and action plan

Do

5. Implement the solution

Check

6. Review and evaluate the results

Act

7. Reflect and act on learnings

Contents

Acknowledgments .... *iii*

How to use *The Problem Solving Memory Jogger™* ...... *iv*

What do the different icons mean? .... *v*

Snapshot of the 7-Step Model .... *vi*

Introduction .... *ix*

Chapter One
Finding & Solving Problems
in Your Processes **1**

Problem solving: an overview 1

Work as a process 2

What is problem solving? 3

What is process improvement? 5

Why are process measures important? 5

What is good team-based problem solving for
process improvement? 7

Key success factors for problem solving 7

Chapter Two
Using a Systematic Model
to Solve Your Problems **11**

What is the power of the Plan-Do-Check-Act
Cycle? 11

What is the 7-Step Model for problem solving? 14

Why is this problem-solving model better
and different from other models? 15

A quick guide to the 7-Step Model: steps,
key tasks, and tools 16

Chapter Three

Implementing the 7-Step
Problem-Solving Model 19

Plan

Step 1. Describe the problem 20

Step 2. Describe the current process 36

Step 3. Identify and verify the root cause(s) 45

Step 4. Develop a solution and action plan 62

Do

Step 5. Implement the solution 92

Check

Step 6. Review and evaluate 101

Act

Step 7. Reflect and act on learnings 114

Chapter Four

Creating a Storyboard 121

Appendix A: Types of Measures 135

Appendix B: Advanced Techniques Resource List .. 137

Appendix C: Control Charts—Recognizing
Sources of Variation 140

Index 157

Introduction

Today, virtually every organization is seeking to ensure that their processes provide the highest attainable product and service quality while making the most efficient use of available resources. To meet this challenge, businesses, government agencies, educational institutions, and not-for-profit organizations are integrating a system of practices known collectively as Process Management.

As defined by GOAL/QPC and used in this book, Process Management is "the never-ending quest for improving business processes by *understanding, measuring, innovating, improving* and *managing* how work gets done to accomplish organizational goals." GOAL/QPC's research has identified five distinct elements that comprise an effective process management system. These elements are:

- **Customer Focus** - defining customer requirements and consistently meeting them and delighting the customer by providing exciting dimensions of quality.

- **Benchmarking** - studying best operating practices and using that knowledge to create visions and goals for higher levels of performance.

- **Process Mapping** - creating clean and efficient steps, guidelines, operating procedures, and decision systems for accomplishing the necessary and sufficient work to meet customer needs and exceeding their expectations.

- **Process Measurement** - creating systems to monitor and report on how well actual performance compares with planned performance and using that data to identify problems and successes.

- **Problem Solving** - a systematic methodology for examining the workings of a process to correct performance deficiencies, and to improve processes and attain even higher levels of performance.

As we enter the 21st century, there is a clear trend in organizations to rely on their employees to help manage business processes and reach performance goals and provide value to customers. Their analytical skills help integrate knowledge of customer requirements into the design of lean and effective processes and to measure the performance of these processes. Their skill in using a systematic method for problem solving empowers them to implement corrective measures when problems occur, to continuously improve the performance of their processes, and to standardize and hold the gain once improvements are made.

The Problem Solving Memory Jogger™ gives employees, at all levels, a proven and practical seven-step, problem-solving method that can easily be learned and used to remove barriers to higher levels of performance and, when necessary, to implement corrective measures.

Whatever your performance improvement goal, *The Problem Solving Memory Jogger*™ will help.

We wish you well in your quest.

Finding & Solving Problems in Your Processes

Problem solving: an overview

We all have to deal with problems in our lives. At work, problem solving is often focused on processes that need to be improved to exceed customer expectations or to improve the efficiency of operations.

In an organizational sense, problems exist when there is a gap between a current condition (what is) and what must be, should be, or could be. In today's turbulent organizations, the "should be" of today may become tomorrow's "must be."

Individuals, teams, and organizations must quickly meet changing customer needs or adjust to a changing business environment that creates a gap between current capabilities and a desired level of functioning.

Problems are solved most effectively when you take a systematic approach. As organizations strive to attain ever-increasing levels of effectiveness and product quality, they find that systematic problem solving is a core competency that must be mastered throughout the organization.

Successful people and successful organizations are not without problems. They simply know how to solve problems and implement effective and lasting corrective measures when they appear.

Work as a process

For you and your team to practice effective problem solving, it's important to understand that a process:

- Is the work you do
- Can be broken down into a repeatable sequence of events
- Consists of connected events that lead to predictable results

A process is the set of procedures or patterns of tasks that you do to produce a product or service that is needed by the customers of the process. If you begin with a known customer need or requirement, a process starts with the **supplier**. A supplier is any person, department, or unit that provides you with **inputs** (information, products, services, or materials that you consume or add value to) in order to accomplish your work (produce an **output**). The **customer** is anyone who has a need and receives or benefits from the output of your work.

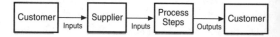

In the series of process steps that you perform, each step is influenced by many factors (equipment, people, measures, materials, policies, and environment) that can affect the outcome of your work.

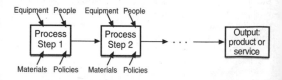

If the process is properly defined (i.e., has a logical sequence of process steps), and the factors work together well, then the outcomes will be good and will satisfy your customers' wants or needs. If any of the factors don't work well together, then the outcomes will not likely satisfy the customer, and the customer may look for another provider for the product or service.

What is problem solving?

A problem exists when there is a gap between the current performance level of a process, product, or service, and the desired performance level. Problem solving, as it's covered in this book, is the systematic investigation of a process to identify the root cause of the gap, and taking corrective action to eliminate the gap and keep it from occurring in the future. To improve a performance gap, you can do any of the following:

- **Fix the process** when it is broken, i.e., it is not meeting the current customer requirement or need (but it did in the past). The gap can occur suddenly or evolve gradually over time.

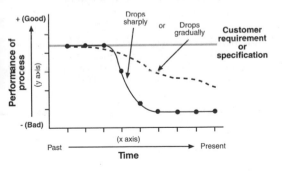

- **Improve the process** when the organization or your customers will benefit from improving it, even though the process is working adequately.

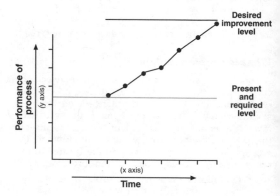

- **Create a new process** because the old one is no longer adequate, or there is no process in place and one needs to be created to fulfill a requirement or need.

You can solve problems successfully by taking a systematic approach to studying your processes. By using helpful tools and techniques, you can analyze and understand what is going on in your process and identify the most important problem to work on.

It is important that you work on the right problem: one that is important to you, your organization, and your customers. Working on the wrong problem will only waste valuable resources and disappoint your customers.

What is process improvement?

You can keep your customers happy by providing them with the "best" possible product or services. "Best" is defined as meeting the customers' needs and exceeding their expectations.

You can provide the best products or services only by improving the *processes* that produce them—by *process improvement*. You do not improve a process by weeding out the good from the bad once a product or service is produced. To do so would only encourage continued production of bad product and raise the cost of the process.

Instead, process improvement is about improving quality while reducing cost and eliminating waste.

To effect an improvement in a process, it's important to have measures of the process. These measures will indicate how the process is performing relative to your organization's desired or targeted performance levels. These measures will help you to **check** your current performance and to focus your corrective or improvement **actions**.

Process improvement may mean making a process more efficient, less costly, more "capable" of meeting customer requirements or specifications, and/or more consistent and reliable in producing an output that is valuable to the customer.

Why are process measures important?

Process measures are a means of determining the degree to which your process activities and their results are conforming to your plan and to customers' requirements and needs.

Measures are important because they provide data that helps teams to identify and solve problems. Measures are also central to defining a problem, understanding how to solve it, and then informing the team and others in the organization on how well the solution is working toward resolving the problem. In short, measures are important indicators for the health of a process. They help you answer the following questions:

- Is the process performing well?
- Is it meeting the customer need or requirement?
- If not, how far off is it?

There are many measures that will help you understand how your process is performing. For example:

Input measures (measure quality, cost, and conformity to requirements)

- **Information, materials, and/or services that you receive from a supplier.** Defective input from a supplier will adversely affect the overall quality of your output and/or process efficiency.

Process measures (measure different elements within the process)

- **Cycle time**: How much time do various steps in the process take? Are there delays in some steps?
- **Bottlenecks**: What types of bottlenecks are you seeing? How frequently? How long is the delay?
- **Quality**: What types of defects are you seeing in a step?

Outcome Measures (measure the final outcome of the process)

- **Yield**: How many of your products or services out of the total that were made or delivered meet customer requirements?
- **Quality**: Does the product or service meet the customer requirements?
- **Cost**: How much does it cost to produce the product or service and how does the cost compare to your competitor's costs?

- **Customer satisfaction**: How happy are your customers with the product or service?

What is good team-based problem solving for process improvement?

Typically, problem-solving and process-improvement activities involve several disciplines and cut vertically, horizontally, or diagonally across several functional areas. For these reasons, most organizational problem-solving efforts are team-based.

Good Teams:
- ✔ Understand work as a process
- ✔ Identify important problems to work on
- ✔ Develop team skills
- ✔ Find the root cause
- ✔ Generate innovative solutions

In order to have a high-performing team, make sure everyone understands his or her role and responsibilities in the team. (Guidelines for teams can be found in the book, *The Team Memory Jogger™*.)

Key success factors for problem solving

Team Membership: Having the right team members is a critical success factor in participative problem solving. While there is no magic formula for successful teams, here are some questions to consider in forming a problem-solving team:

- Does the team have the right knowledge, skills, and experience?
- Are all perspectives on the issue represented? (i.e., customer, stakeholder)
- Is the size of the team manageable?

- Are temporary members with specialized skills needed?
- Can team members devote the time necessary to work on the project?
- Does the team have a leader?
- Does the team have a healthy mix of experienced and inexperienced problem solvers as members?

Team Environment: The benefits of working in a team environment allow each team member to:

- Contribute ideas based on his or her knowledge and experience
- Think creatively
- Learn by collecting, sharing, and analyzing data
- Develop the interpersonal skills vital to effective teamwork

Collectively, these conditions will allow a team to generate not only more ideas but better ideas that will lead them toward finding better solutions.

Team Commitment: A team that is committed to effective problem solving will take the time to establish clear goals and team procedures, learn how to apply the tools and steps of the 7-Step Model, develop and recruit strong leadership skills, document their work every step of the way, and support one another.

Clear goals and objectives

- Define the problem's boundaries. Which processes are involved? Which are not?
- Put together the right people to solve the problem.
- Establish measures of end results (goal).
- Develop a plan of how the team will accomplish the goal, including appropriate timelines and deadlines.

Knowledge of how to apply the 7-Step Model and the basic tools for problem solving

Some of these tools are:

- The Quality Control Tools (e.g., Run Chart, Pareto Chart, Control Chart, Flowchart, Cause and Effect Diagram)
- The Management and Planning Tools (e.g., Affinity and Tree Diagram)
- The Creativity Tools (e.g., Imaginary Brainstorming, Picture and Word Associations)

Strong, effective, and efficient leadership

- Train, motivate, and guide teams.
- Develop leadership among all members.
- Act as a liaison between the team and others in the organization, especially with management.
- Apply good team meeting skills, which include:
    - Assigning roles and responsibilities
    - Using agendas and keeping to time allocations of each item
    - Soliciting active participation of every team member
    - Promoting active listening, constructive feedback, and clear communication
    - Establishing and living by team ground rules
- For more information on team facilitation guidelines, refer to the pocket guide *Facilitation at a Glance!*

Decision-making procedures

- Use consensus rather than majority vote. It's important that all team members support the decision of the team.

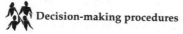 **Documentation of the team's work**

- Plan and record the project as a team.
- Give periodic team reports to the right people.
- Use the tools to document the team's discussions.
- Share minutes of team meetings as appropriate.

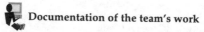 **Visible, committed sponsorship and recognition**

- Nurture a supportive and creative environment.
- Give the team a sense of ownership of the problem.
- Provide guidance and parameters for the team to work within.
- Give both verbal and active commitment, i.e., "walk the talk."
- Work to build trust among team members, managers, and others in the organization.
- Provide needed resources, including time, meeting space, and materials.
- Recognize individuals for their contributions toward the team's success.

Chapter Two

Using a Systematic Model to Solve Your Problems

An effective and systematic approach to problem solving is to use the 7-Step Model, which provides a repeatable set of steps, actions, and tools as part of the Plan-Do-Check-Act Cycle.

What is the power of the Plan-Do-Check-Act (PDCA) Cycle?

The PDCA Cycle was a fundamental component of Dr. W. Edwards Deming's pioneering work in quality management. He saw work as a never-ending improvement process to achieve better quality products and services and to improve the processes that make and deliver them. The PDCA Cycle, or "Deming Cycle" as it is often called, consists of four stages: Plan, Do, Check, Act.

The PDCA Cycle is a powerful approach for problem solving. It is an excellent foundation for helping teams to:

- Systematically identify and understand a problem or issue and its root cause(s) rather than the symptoms
- Generate ideas and develop an effective plan to solve the problem
- Ensure that the current problem stays fixed and then move on to other problems

The PDCA Cycle can be compared to the scientific method many of us learned in high school or college science classes, i.e., create a hypothesis, perform an experiment, analyze the results, and draw conclusions.

The PDCA Cycle provides, as does the scientific method, the principles and procedures for the systematic pursuit of knowledge. Using the PDCA Cycle will provide teams with the knowledge they need to fix, improve, or create any product, service, or work process.

The steps of the PDCA Cycle are:

PLAN...   Plan a change or a test aimed at improvement, once the root cause of the problem is determined.

DO...   Carry out the change or the test, preferably in a pilot or on a small scale.

CHECK...   Check to see if the desired result was achieved, what or if anything went wrong, and what was learned.

ACT...   Adopt the change if the desired result was achieved. If the results are not as desired, repeat the cycle using knowledge accumulated from the previous cycle.

In applying the PDCA Cycle to problem solving and process improvement, it is assumed that:

- A process exists
- Goals, objectives, and requirements for the inputs, process steps, and outputs have been established
- Key performance measures have been established and applied

The problem-solving process normally begins at the **Check** stage where actual performance is measured and compared with performance requirements. When the results indicate a gap between the measure and the required performance, and the gap is severe enough to cause you to **Act** (to repeat the process), you are ready to begin applying the 7-Step Model for problem solving.

Another of Deming's major contributions was the Control Chart. (See Appendix C for detailed information on this tool.) The Control Chart is very helpful in process improvement because it identifies what problems are due to common causes (sources of random variation that are inherent in the normal operation of the process), and which problems are due to special causes (unique events that are not associated with the normal operation of the process).

Deming had three important lessons on variation in a process:

1. Fix special causes first, then concentrate on common causes.

2. Always distinguish between what the customer requires from your process, i.e., the specification limits, and what the process actually produces when it's "in control," i.e., within control limits.

3. It is almost always beneficial to the process owner and process customer if you reduce variation in your process. Reducing this variation will help you to achieve six sigma quality, which means 3.4 defects per one million outputs.

What is the 7-Step Model for problem solving?

 While the PDCA Cycle maps out a fundamental approach to understanding and resolving problems, teams often need more detail to guide them in their problem-solving effort. Team members often ask, "What do I do in the **Plan** stage?" "What tools are most helpful in understanding the problem and getting at the root causes?" or "What is the best solution and how do I implement it?"

Each step in the 7-Step Model explains what must be done and the typical tool(s) used. These steps are based on the PDCA Cycle.

The steps and key tasks in the 7-Step Model are defined in the table on pages 16–18. The table also recommends which tools are most appropriate for each step of the model. Because of space constraints, only a few of the recommended tools are described in this book. For detailed instructions on constructing a tool, consult the following pocket guides:

- *The Memory Jogger™ II* (Affinity Diagram, Brainstorming, Cause and Effect Diagram, Control Chart, Flowchart, Gantt Chart, Matrix Diagram, Pareto Chart, Process Decision Program Chart, Radar Chart, Run Chart, Tree Diagram)
- *The Creativity Tools Memory Jogger™* (Classic Brainstorming and Imaginary Brainstorming)
- *The Project Management Memory Jogger™* (Project or Action Plan)

Why is this problem-solving model better and different from other models?

Teams have often learned the tools apart from the context of a problem-solving situation. The 7-Step Model presented in this book provides this context. The presentation of this model provides teams with a step-by-step approach to problem solving, includes sub-steps with recommended tools for doing each of the seven steps, and illustrates a case example that is introduced throughout each step and tool application. As your team follows the steps in the model, you'll discover that:

- Each step is specific in recommending actions that need to be accomplished.
- In some places, there are checklists to help you navigate through the step, making it easier to know what you need to do, what you've done, and what you still need to do.
- Each step focuses on the most basic tool(s) required to accomplish the step, including helpful tips that will enhance the team's construction and interpretation of the tools.
- When a team wants or is ready to expand beyond the basic tools, there is the option of integrating more of the management and planning tools, the creativity tools, or other helpful tips. Check out "How do I turbo-charge this step?" to find out more.

A Quick Guide to the 7-Step Model: Steps, Key Tasks, and Tools

Step	Key Tasks	Primary Tools
Plan		
1. Describe the problem.	• Look for changes in important business performance measures. • Assemble and support the right team. • Narrow down the project focus. • Write a final problem statement.	• Control Chart • Pareto Chart • Run Chart
2. Describe the current process.	• Create a Flowchart of the current process. • Validate the Flowchart and the performance measures with the owners, users, and customers of the current process.	• Flowchart
3. Identify and verify the root cause(s).	• Construct the Cause & Effect Diagram. • Review the Cause & Effect Diagram. • Determine if more data will clarify the problem. • Select the root cause(s). • Verify the root cause(s).	• Classic Brainstorming • Cause & Effect Diagram • Matrix Diagram

© 2000 GOAL/QPC

Step	Key Tasks	Primary Tools
Plan *(continued)*		
4. Develop a solution and action plan.	• Generate potential solutions. • Rank potential solutions; select the best solution. • Generate possible tasks for the solution. • Construct a detailed action plan.	• Affinity Diagram • Gantt Chart • Decision Matrix or Prioritization Matrices • Process Decision Program Chart • Responsibility Matrix • Tree Diagram
Do		
5. Implement the solution.	• Communicate the plan. • Meet regularly to share information on how the implementation is going.	• Action Plan • Selected measurement tools
Check		
6. Review and evaluate.	• Review the results of the change. • Revise the process as necessary. • Standardize the improvement. • Continue to monitor the process for changes.	• Control Chart • Pareto Chart • Run Chart

Continued on next page

Step	Key Tasks	Primary Tools
Act		
7. Reflect and act on learnings.	• Assess the problem-solving process the team used and the results achieved; recommend changes, if needed. • Continue the improvement process where needed; standardize where possible. • Celebrate success.	• Radar Chart

Note: While there are many more tools available than are listed in the table, the purpose of the 7-Step Model is to start with the basics for a team just getting started. Look for the sections called "How do I turbo-charge this step?" in Chapter 3 to get more out of your problem-solving effort.

The seven steps of the model are presented in more detail with a case example in Chapter 3.

Chapter Three

Implementing the 7-Step Problem-Solving Model

This model uses seven discrete steps that are based on the Plan-Do-Check-Act Cycle for problem solving. It helps teams to:

- Systematically solve a problem
- Understand and communicate the problem
- Identify when additional data is needed
- Synthesize data into a visual form that can be analyzed
- Use tools to interpret data and make conclusions
- Develop and implement solutions to the problem
- Monitor the problem for ongoing effectiveness
- Learn from the team's problem-solving experience

Plan   Page
   Step 1. Describe the problem   20
   Step 2. Describe the current process   36
   Step 3. Identify and verify the root cause(s)   45
   Step 4. Develop a solution and action plan   62

Do
   Step 5. Implement the solution   92

Check
   Step 6. Review and evaluate   101

Act
   Step 7. Reflect and act on learnings   114

Step 1

Describe the Problem:

Select the problem that will be addressed first (or next) and describe it clearly.

What does this step do? 🏊

Helps teams to focus on the most important problem rather than a trivial one when resources and time are limited. Teams can then begin to understand and describe the problem and improvement opportunity.

What concepts must I understand to do this step?

Importance of Understanding the Problem

- **Focus on the right problem.** With limited time and resources, it is essential to focus on a problem that is most important to the customer, the team, and the organization.

- **Break the problem into manageable pieces.** This prevents a team from feeling overwhelmed by the larger problem and helps the team identify the pieces that it can control and change.

- **Gain more knowledge to better define the problem.** This ensures the team keeps all its efforts focused on solving the right problem with the right people.

- **Describe the problem as the gap between what "is" and what it should or could be.**

Importance of Gathering Data and Information

Data can help teams:

- **Reveal a problem.** Teams can't fix a problem they don't know about.
- **Describe a problem.** When teams understand what the problem is, they can fix the problem rather than just addressing the symptom.
- **Monitor and control a problem.** Teams can make sure that what they fix or improve stays that way.
- **Prevent a problem.** When there is a consistent trend or cycle in the data, a team can take action to reduce or eliminate the undesired trend or cycle in the process before it becomes critical and/or apparent to the customer. It's always easier to prevent a problem than to have to correct it.

Types of Data

There are two types of data to measure process performance: variable data and attribute data. It is important to know which type of data you have since it helps determine which tool to use.

- **Variable data:** data is measured and plotted on a continuous scale over time, e.g., temperature, cost figures, times, strength, pH levels. Use Run Charts, Histograms, Scatter Diagrams, and Variable Control Charts to illustrate this data.
- **Attribute data:** data is counted and plotted as discrete events for a specified period of time, based on some characteristic, e.g., types of shipping errors, types of customer complaints, reasons for downtime. Use Check Sheets, Pareto Charts, and Attribute Control Charts for this type of data.

What actions must be taken in this step?

- **Identify** important **business and process measures** that focus on the **customer.**
- Identify what **type of data** is needed to define the problem.
- **Arrange data** into a form that can be **analyzed** for meaning. Two good choices are the Run Chart and Pareto Chart.
- **Write a problem statement** that describes the problem as a gap between the present condition (what is) and the required or desired condition (what should be).

How do I do it? 🏃

1. **Look for changes in important business and process performance measures.**

   a) Monitor important processes and their key business performance measures.

   - Measures must:
     - Be objectively measured with data that reflect the process.
     - Support major business objectives.
     - Be directly related to a customer need or financial need of the organization.
   - See the chart on p. 25 for examples of measures.
   - For more ideas on measures, see Types of Measures in Appendix A.
   - Depending on the organizational improvement structure, this step may be done by a steering team, management team, or problem-solving work team.
   - If the business performance measures already exist, monitor them using graphics and charts.

☑ Whenever possible, start with data. The discovery and definition of a problem through data collection and analysis reduces the power of opinions and ill-informed decisions.

☑ Typically a team uses data to determine:
1) Where the problem is and is not occurring;
2) When the problem began; and
3) What the extent of the problem is.

☑ Sometimes the gap between the present and desired condition is so large that emergency actions are needed. These actions may not support the identification of root causes and solutions but can limit the impact of the problem. These actions may include: 1) Recalling product if it threatens someone's safety and health; 2) Quarantining finished product; 3) Stopping further production.

b) Chart the current business and process performance measure(s).

- Use a **Run Chart** or a **Control Chart** to plot variable data. These charts show you how the measure performs over time. (For more information, consult the *MJII*, p. 141 for the Run Chart and Appendix C in this book for the Control Chart.)

  - Data graphed over time helps teams to see if the process they are studying is steady, improving, or getting worse.

- If the process is performing differently than expected, then a team has cause to question this. The team should determine why it has changed and the extent it has changed.

- Use a Control Chart to distinguish between common cause variation (naturally occurring within the process) and special cause variation (a unique cause not naturally occurring within the process).

• In addition to the Run Chart or a Control Chart, a **Pareto Chart** can be used to chart the performance of the business and/or process measure and to prioritize business issues that need to be addressed. Use a Pareto Chart to visually display attribute data. (See Pareto Chart, *MJII*, p. 95.)

- A Pareto Chart helps a team identify the biggest problem or need for improvement by taking a complex issue and breaking it down into categories of different problems that are occurring. It is used to further prioritize problem areas, categorize customer complaints, defect types, etc.

- The Pareto Chart is based on the Pareto principle: 20% of the sources cause 80% of the problems.

- Identify the category that has the highest frequency of occurrence, e.g., the highest cost or highest negative impact, and consider focusing there.

c) Examine the measures and use significant changes in them as signs of potential problems for a team to resolve.

d) Create a draft statement of the problem.

Examples of Key Business Performance Measures

Problem	Measured objectively with data		Supports major business objectives	Directly related to customer need or company finances
	Measure	Chart		
HOSPITAL: Patients waiting too long to see the emergency room physician	Wait time from patient logs	Run, Control, or Histogram	Relates to quality of patient care	Impacts finances if patients go to another hospital
	Reasons for long wait time	Pareto		
PLANT: Manufacturing not meeting production targets	Yields (% of quality)	Run or Control	Efficiency and quality of products	Customers' orders not filled
	Machine downtime (# of times machine breaks and duration)	Run or Histogram		Company loses customers to competitors
	Reasons for downtime	Pareto		Lowers sales

This is the beginning of a case that illustrates the use of the 7-Step Model. The case continues throughout the steps in this chapter.

"The Case of the Missing Deadline"

The Atlantic Book Company (ABC) is a 145-person publishing firm. ABC's success in the last 20 years has been in writing and publishing "how-to" books. More recently, ABC's merger with another publisher has enabled the company to expand into new markets.

Growth has come at a cost, however. As the company has grown, it is increasingly difficult to finish new products on schedule. Jeremy, ABC's New Product Development Manager, was well aware that deadlines were missed more often than met.

Not only was it difficult for Jeremy's new product development staff to meet the deadlines, but morale was suffering too. The latest employee survey showed a 15% drop in job satisfaction. The decline was directly related to work pressure and having to work longer hours.

Jeremy also knew that on-time delivery of new products was an important measure of the health of the business. He decided it was time to solve this problem. Using the data from the Run Chart, Jeremy composed the following problem statement:

"For the past two years, and the last eight projects, book production has been late on average by 7.9 weeks."

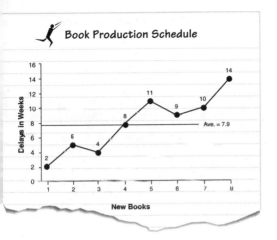

Book Production Schedule

Delays in Weeks (y-axis: 0, 2, 4, 6, 8, 10, 12, 14, 16)

Data points: 1 → 2, 2 → 5, 3 → 4, 4 → 8, 5 → 11, 6 → 9, 7 → 10, 8 → 14

Ave. = 7.9

New Books (x-axis: 1, 2, 3, 4, 5, 6, 7, 8)

2. Assemble and support the right team.

- If a steering team identified the problem area to address, another team should be chartered to further study and solve the problem. (Also see *PMMJ*, pp. 26-27.)
- If a team has already been formed and identified the problem, verify that the team has the right members.
- Consider including suppliers and customers of the process as team members.
- Also include people who will satisfy the team's needs.
- Ask team members if anyone is missing or needed, but remember to keep the team small and manageable, i.e., 5–8 people.

Putting Together an Effective Team

Skills	Does someone do something unique that is a required part of the process? *Examples:* precision welder, secretary, lab technician, or facilitator.
Knowledge	Is there someone who has essential pieces of information about the problem or process? *Examples:* research chemist, nurse, customer and/or supplier, service manager.
Approval	Is there someone whose "OK" is required before a likely solution can be implemented? *Examples:* purchasing manager, finance manager, general manager, CEO.
Acceptance	Are there individuals who can effectively block implementation of a likely solution if it is not acceptable to them? *Examples:* process owner, supervisor, worker, or sales representative.

The ABC Problem-Solving Team

- Jeremy, Manager of New Product Development (needed for Approval, Knowledge)
- Felicia, Lead Editor (needed for Skills, Knowledge)
- Rich, Customer Representative (needed for Acceptance)
- Lani, Primary Writer (needed for Skills, Knowledge)
- Stephano, Copy Layout (needed for Skills)

At each team meeting, Rich took notes and documented the key ideas that were presented so the team could develop an ongoing storyboard to be posted outside the lunchroom. (Storyboards are discussed in Chapter 4.)

---

3. **Narrow down the project focus.**

a) Look for any other data opportunities to further understand and clarify the problem.

- Is there a different process measure that should be studied?

- Is there additional data that would help you understand the largest bar on the Pareto Chart?

- Do you need to create a new Run Chart on a critical measure?

- Would it be helpful to talk to customers? Suppliers?

✔️ Customers' input is invaluable! Their insights to the problem may change what you choose to measure and how you measure it in the process. Understanding your customers' needs can influence the type of solution you later put into place.

✔️ Sometimes you can narrow the scope of the original problem, depending on the knowledge of your team members and the data that you've collected. Keep the scope of the problem within your team's:

- Area of control or influence
- Budget
- Schedule for implementing a solution

b) As a team, look at the data gathered so far. Begin to ask, "What's wrong?" "What's not working?" List all potential issues, problems, and opportunities.

c) Identify the issue to focus on. Consider these questions when selecting the issue:

- What issue appears to be the most important one in need of changing or improving? Look at the Run Chart or Pareto Chart.

- Is that issue the most important one to the customer? The team? The organization?

- Does the team have control over the part of the process that needs to be changed?

- Will the necessary resources be available to address this problem?

© 2000 GOAL/QPC

ABC Team Narrows Down the Project Focus

The team members decided they had to narrow the focus of the problem before they could find a possible solution. They collected data on the past eight projects by talking with other employees, looking at past records, and studying time logs.

After reviewing this data, the team listed possible reasons for the delays. Then the team collected data from project history files on how often each type of delay had occurred. With this data, the team constructed a Pareto Chart to show the frequency of delays.

Reasons for Project Delays

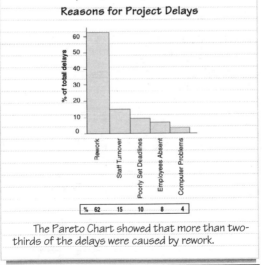

| % | 62 | 15 | 10 | 8 | 4 |

The Pareto Chart showed that more than two-thirds of the delays were caused by rework.

The team dug a little deeper by reviewing work assignment sheets and time logs for the last eight projects completed. Using data from that search, the team named the reasons why projects were delayed and created a second Pareto Chart that showed where the greatest number of delays were occurring.

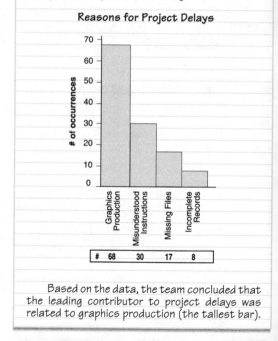

Reasons for Project Delays

| # | 68 | 30 | 17 | 8 |

Based on the data, the team concluded that the leading contributor to project delays was related to graphics production (the tallest bar).

4. Write a final problem statement.

- Write a clear and concise statement of the problem to be addressed by the team.
- A good problem statement will include the four components shown in the table below.

Components of a Good Problem Statement

1. Direction	What do you want to do to the performance level of the process, *e.g.*, *increase, decrease, cut back, improve, expand, develop, remove, reduce, lower, eliminate, shorten, extend.*
2. Business Measure	The key measure for the process under study, *e.g.*, *errors, mistakes, breakdowns, yields, availability, turnaround time, timeliness, wait time, accuracy, cycle time.*
3. Performance Measure	The current numeric performance value of the business measure.
4. Process Name	The process under study.

ABC Team's
Final Problem Statement

" Reduce the large number of graphics needing rework in the new product development process so that book production schedules can be met on time."

How can I turbo-charge this step? ⚡➔

The key to a successful problem-solving effort is to get a team off to a good start with the right people working on the right problem. Consider these other approaches to identifying and defining the *right* problem.

Affinity Diagram and Interrelationship Digraph
(MJII, p. 12 and 76.)

1. Start by talking to the customers, suppliers, or staff and workers. Identify their issues and organize them using the Affinity Diagram. This method truly focuses on a customer-identified concern!

2. Identify the driver of these themed groupings using the Interrelationship Digraph.

3. Identify a key business performance measure related to the driver.

4. Construct a Run Chart or Control Chart on the measure. Construct a Pareto Chart on the identified types of concerns/issues.

Problem Reformulation Tool *(CTMJ, p. 97.)*

If a team has trouble identifying the problem, this tool can help a team visualize the problem in a new way.

1. Using pictures, questions, and criteria, identify the components of the system (process) in order to identify new approaches to focusing on the right problem and then solving it.

2. Look at how the components affect the system and at the interrelationships between the components.

3. After writing new statements of how the components or relationships relate back to the original problem, prioritize and select one.

4. Identify a measure on this new problem statement and evaluate it for further study.

Purpose Hierarchy Tool *(CTMJ, p. 119.)*

This tool identifies the full range of possible purposes of an improvement effort and then focuses in on the one that fits the needs of the customer and available resources.

1. Brainstorm a list of purpose statements that begin with the word "to" and have an action (verb) and an object of that action.

2. Code each statement as to its level of difficulty.

   S   = simple
   SM = simple to medium
   M   = medium
   MC = medium to complex
   C   = complex

3. Order the statements from simple to complex and then select the focus purpose by mapping the statements against applicable criteria.

Step 2

Describe the Current Process:

Describe the current process surrounding the improvement opportunity.

What does this step do? 🏃•

Helps a team to understand work as a process and to identify where in the process the problem occurs.

What concepts must I understand to do this step?

Customer and Supplier Relationships

Each step in a process creates relationships in which people depend on each other to get work done. Each process step depends on one or more suppliers to provide products, materials, services, and/or information that are:

- Reliable
- Defect or error free
- On time
- Complete

In exchange, at each process step the customer provides suppliers with:

- Requirements that are clearly stated
- Timely feedback when needs are not being met

© 2000 GOAL/QPC

Process Documentation May Be Outdated

Teams need to understand the process they are trying to improve. Oftentimes, a current and detailed Flowchart doesn't exist. If the process has never been documented or the existing Flowchart is outdated, the team will either need to create a Flowchart or update the old one.

Every Process is a System

It's important for everyone in the process to look at and treat it as a system of connected pieces. If you change even one part of the system, it will always affect how the whole system works (or doesn't work).

What actions must be taken in this step?

- **Construct, update,** and/or **interpret** a **Flowchart** to describe and study work as a process.
- **Identify** the **value, time,** and **cost** added **for each step** in the process.

How do I do it?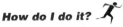

1. **Create a Flowchart of the current process.**
   - Use a Flowchart to show all of the tasks and decisions involved in implementing the current process. (See *MJII*, pp. 56–62.)
   - Use symbols to show the flow of actions and decisions in a process from start to end.
   - List all of the steps of the process **as they are currently done**. Keep the level of detail as simple as possible. If necessary, you can always add more detailed steps later.

Flowchart Symbols

Oval ⬭	Shows the materials, information, or action (inputs) that start the process, and the results (output) at the end of the process.
Box □	Shows an activity performed in the process. Although multiple arrows may come into each box, usually only one arrow leaves each box.
Diamond ◇	Shows those points in the process where a yes/no question is being asked or a decision is required.
Circle with Letter or Number (A)	Identifies a break in the Flowchart and is continued elsewhere on the same page or another page.
Arrow →	Shows the flow of the process.

> ✔ Unless you're using flowcharting software, write each step on a Post-it™ Note. The steps can then be easily sequenced and rearranged.

ABC Team
Flowcharts the Process

Lani, the main writer, and Felicia, the lead editor, said that the current process wasn't clear to them.

Stephano said it seemed like projects were getting more complex, and paperwork and files were getting lost as they were shuttled between steps and people in the process.

The team created a Flowchart of the entire process to make sense of what was really happening.

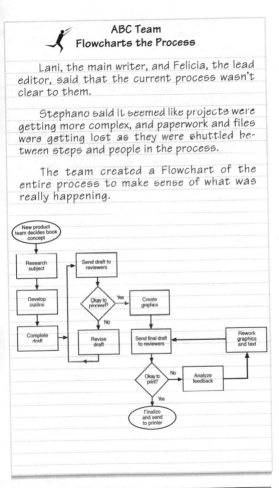

2. **Validate the Flowchart and the performance measures with the owners, users, and customers of the current process.**

   • Before teams can improve a process, they need to understand it. The people who have this understanding are those who work on some part of the process or who use the information, products, or services that are produced by it.

Check for . . .	By asking . . .
Completeness	Does the Flowchart show all of the critical tasks and decision points?
Accuracy	Do the words in the Flowchart clearly describe what's happening at each step and decision point? Are all of the connections drawn as they actually happen, especially flowing from decision points?
Time spent*	What's the range of time that it takes to complete each task or to make each decision?
Overall process measures*	How does the person responsible for the overall process measure its success? How does the customer of the process measure its success? Are the measures objective (based on facts) or subjective (based on opinions)?
Sub-step measures*	How does the person responsible for each sub-step measure its success? How does the customer of each sub-step measure its success? Are the measures objective (based on facts) or subjective (based on opinions)?

Continued on next page

Check for . . .	By asking . . .
Bottlenecks and delays*	Are there delays because the criteria for making decisions are unclear? Are there inspection points where a lot of products and services are rejected or diverted?
Responsibilities	Who measures, improves, and provides information about each step? Is there one person ultimately responsible for each step or is it a shared responsibility?
Quality problems*	Are there any recorded customer complaints about a particular step in the process? Are there any steps that are reworking products, services, or information because they don't meet customer needs?

*Any of these categories can be used to identify areas to work on in your organization's continuous improvement efforts.

- Confirm the accuracy of the process as it is drawn in the Flowchart and the time estimates for each step by letting the process run untouched.
- Identify the value, time, and cost added for each step in the process.

A step adds time and/or cost when:

- A product or service needs to be inspected.

- A product can't move further in the process because a decision hasn't been made, information hasn't been provided, or related process steps haven't been finished.

- Anything is reworked.

- A product moves anywhere other than the next step in the process.

A step adds value when:

- It makes a product more useful to the customer.

- A customer would be willing to pay for the activity in that step.

- It is required to make the product function properly when used by the customer.

ABC Team Validates Flowchart and Performance Measures of Current Process

Team members validated the Flowchart by reviewing it with coworkers, customers, and suppliers. (They used the same criteria as those listed in the table on pages 40 and 41.) They all agreed that the Flowchart was on target.

How can I turbo-charge this step? ✏️➡️

Top-down Flowchart *(MJII, p. 60.)*

If team members need a deeper look at one or more steps within the process, they can use a Top-down Flowchart. This enables teams to examine in greater detail what activities and decisions take place while performing a step. Follow these instructions to create a Top-down Flowchart:

1. Construct a Macro Flowchart of the major steps and decisions in your process. (Use the symbols shown on page 38.)
2. Assign a number to each step.
3. For each major step, list the sub-steps and their supporting sub-steps. Use a numbered outline system to show the order and hierarchy of the sub-steps.
4. Review the list of sub-steps to identify ways to simplify the process and eliminate bottlenecks and delays.

Research Subject Area

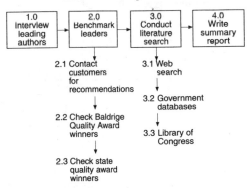

Deployment Flowchart (*MJII, p. 61.*)

Use a Deployment Flowchart to clarify roles and responsibilities, track accountability, and determine if the most appropriate staff resources are being used to perform the steps. Follow these instructions to create a Deployment Flowchart:

1. List the names of the individuals or departments that perform different tasks in the process across the top of a sheet of paper or flipchart paper.

2. Using a Macro Flowchart of the major steps and decisions in your process, place each action step (box) and decision point (diamond) below the name of the individual or department that performs the task or makes the decision.

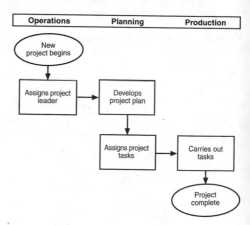

Step 3

Identify and Verify the Root Cause(s):

Describe all of the possible causes of the problem and agree on the root cause(s).

Plan

Act

Do

Check

What does this step do?

Helps teams identify all the possible causes contributing to the problem and agree on the root causes in order to reduce or eliminate them.

What concepts must I understand to do this step?

Relationship of Cause and Effect

To get at the heart of a problem, teams need to identify all the possible causes of some effect (the problem). Causes are usually attributed to variation in how work gets done. Variation can occur in materials, equipment, and methods, or in the way people do their jobs.

- Variation can occur in one or more process steps.
- The more variation that occurs, the more the effect is influenced and deviates from the desired output.
- To solve a problem, a team needs to identify the source of variation before taking corrective action.
- Sources of variation can be grouped into two major classes:

  - **Common cause** is a source of variation that is always present; part of the random variation inherent in the process itself. Its origin can usually be traced to an element of the process that only management can correct.

- **Special cause** is a source that is intermittent, localized, seasonal, unpredictable, unstable. Its origin can usually be traced to an element of the system that can be corrected locally, that is, an employee or operator may be able to correct a special cause.

Root Cause Analysis

Root cause analysis is a process of tracking down the sources of variation to identify the key sources that are causing the problem. These root causes, when eliminated or changed, will make the biggest impact toward solving the problem.

- Root cause analysis involves creative thought, data collection, analysis, and objective reasoning.
- Problem-solving teams are most effective when they use a standard approach to identifying root causes.

What actions must be taken in this step?

- **Identify** all possible **causes** of the problem.
- Construct a **Cause and Effect Diagram.**
- **Select** the **root cause(s).**
- **Verify** the root cause(s) **with data.**

How do I do it?

1. **Construct the Cause & Effect Diagram.**

   - A Cause and Effect Diagram helps teams to create a picture of the possible causes of a problem; understand how the causes are related, and think about why the problem occurs and where it's occurring.
   - a) Using flipchart or butcher paper, write the problem statement on the right-hand side of the paper and draw a box around it. Also draw a long line

with a large arrow pointing to it. Make sure everyone on the team agrees on the wording of the problem statement. Add as much information as possible on the "what," "where," "when," and "how much" of the problem.

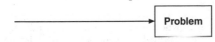

b) Develop a list of factors that could be causing or contributing to the problem.

- Ask, "What are all the possible causes of the problem?"
- Record the answers on Post it™ Notes or cards.

c) Select the major cause categories that are appropriate for the team's diagram. There are two types of categories.

- **Major Cause Categories** (Also known as Dispersion Analysis Type. See *MJII*, p. 23.)

  These are standard categories that are generic to most problems. Use either the 4 M's or 4 P's or a combination of them to develop your major cause categories.

  – The 4 M's: Machines, Methods, Materials, Manpower/People.
  – The 4 P's: Policies, Procedures, People, Plant/Equipment.

- **Major Process Steps** (Also known as Process Classification Type. See *MJII*, p. 24.)

  These are the major steps of the process in which the problem is occurring. A team can review the Flowchart of the process to determine the key steps.

☑ There is no perfect set or number of categories. Select the categories that best fit the team's situation and needs.

☑ The Affinity Diagram can be useful for teams who are having trouble determining the most appropriate major cause categories. Basic instructions for the Affinity Diagram are: a) Brainstorm 10–20 causes; b) Sort the causes into related groupings; c) Create header cards and use them as the major cause categories on the Cause and Effect Diagram.

• Write the major cause categories (or major process steps) on the flipchart paper. Draw a box around each category and connect it with a line and arrow that points toward the line extending out from the problem statement.

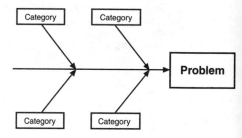

d) Place the Post-it™ Notes or cards of possible causes in the appropriate cause categories of the diagram.

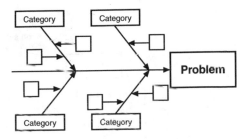

A cause may be placed in as many categories as it seems to fit.

e) Create the next levels of causes.

- For each cause listed on the diagram, ask "Why does this happen?" For each response, repeat the same question and write down the next response. Each successive answer is another possible cause.

- List the team's responses as branches off of the major causes. The placement of connecting lines shows the logical relationship of each response to the one that preceded it.

- Continue to question "Why?" for each cause until the team decides it has enough information to identify the root cause.

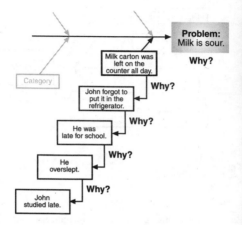

Problem: Milk is sour.

Why?

Milk carton was left on the counter all day.

Why?

John forgot to put it in the refrigerator.

Why?

He was late for school.

Why?

He overslept.

Why?

John studied late.

Category

Two guidelines for knowing when to stop asking "Why?" are: 1) The team has asked "Why?" to five levels of detail, and 2) The cause is controlled by more than one level of management removed from the team.

The ABC Team Constructs the Cause & Effect Diagram

The team's ideas for why so many of the graphics were reworked are shown on the Post-it™ Notes below.

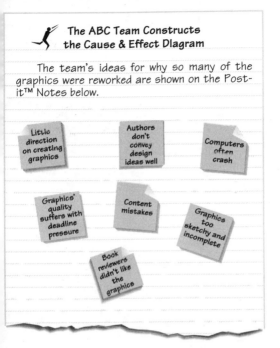

Part of the ABC team's Cause & Effect Diagram is shown below.

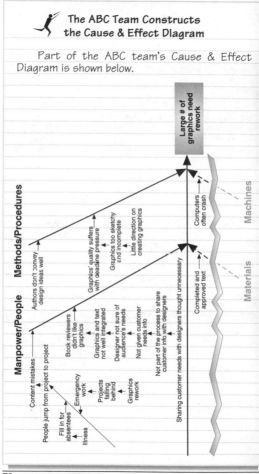

2. Review the Cause & Effect Diagram.

- Use the checklist below to review the accuracy and completeness of the team's diagram.

Ask:	If you answer no, then ...
Is the problem (effect) correctly stated? Does it include the name of the process?	• Rewrite the problem statement. Compare the statement written in Step 1 and include any new information gathered.
Have you listed all the potential causes?	• Ask others who also know the process to identify possible causes.
Are all the brainstormed causes categorized?	• If you have trouble fitting a brainstormed cause into a category, add another category called "Other" and place the cause there.
Have you identified solutions instead of causes?	• Save these on a list of possible solutions for later. For now, focus only on identifying causes.
Do the causes relate to the issue?	• Have the team reread the problem statement (effect) again. So as not to lose any information, place any unrelated items in a "parking lot" list to address later.
Is the diagram complete and understandable?	• Make sure every category has detail on it. • Explain any jargon. • Make sure all the causes, as they are written in the diagram, are clearly understood so that their meaning can be recalled later by any team member.

3. Determine if more data will clarify the problem.

- Many of the causes identified by team members are known causes, while others may be informed guesses. Whenever possible, validate these guesses by collecting and analyzing data.
- Use the tool that will best illustrate the type of data you plan to collect.

Tool	Use it to . . .	MJII page
Check Sheet/ Pareto Chart	• Validate how frequently a cause occurs.	31/95
Control Chart	• Determine if the process where the cause occurs is stable and predictable. • Identify when special cause variations occur.	36
Histogram	• Show the centering and variation of the process due to a cause.	66
Pareto Chart	• Focus attention on the problem areas that have the greatest potential for improvement.	95
Process Capability	• Determine if a process is consistently producing outputs (products/services) that meet customer requirements.	132
Run Chart	• See how the process performs over time due to a cause. Also, to find trends, cycles, or shifts that may occur related to an identified cause.	141
Scatter Diagram	• Determine relationships between multiple causes (variables) and how they influence the effect.	145

4. Select the root cause(s).

a) Identify likely candidates for the root cause(s) by one or more of the following actions:

- Look for causes that appear repeatedly within or across major cause or process categories.
- Look for changes and other sources of variation in the process or the environment.
- Use consensus decision-making methods such as Nominal Group Technique or Multivoting. (See *MJII*, p. 91 and 93, respectively.)
- Use collected data that substantiates a potential root cause.
- Use discussion and logic to convincingly explain how a cause is creating the problem.

b) Select the root cause(s) from the list of identified root causes.

☑ Highlight, box, or circle the identified root cause(s) so they stand out on the Cause & Effect Diagram.

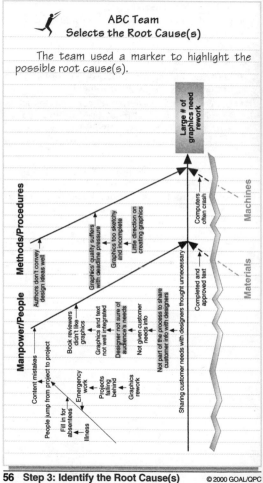

ABC Team
Selects the Root Cause(s)

The team used a marker to highlight the possible root cause(s).

Large # of graphics need rework

Methods/Procedures
- Authors don't convey design ideas well
- Graphics quality suffers with deadline pressure
- Graphics too sketchy and incomplete
- Little direction on creating graphics

Machines
- Computers often crash

Manpower/People
- Content mistakes
- People jump from project to project
- Fill in for absentees
- Illness
- Emergency work
- Projects falling behind
- Graphics rework
- Book reviewers didn't like graphics
- Graphics and text not well integrated
- Designer not sure of audience's needs
- Not given customer needs info
- Not part of the process to share customer info with designers
- Sharing customer needs with designers thought unnecessary

Materials
- Completed and approved text

© 2000 GOAL/QPC

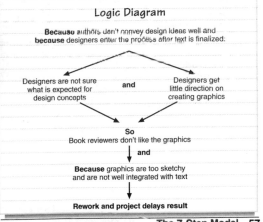

ABC Team
Selects the Root Cause(s), continued

Now the team looked for ways to logically describe how one or more ideas could be the root cause(s). Felicia noticed that "too sketchy," "little direction on creating graphics," and "authors don't convey design ideas well" were related to book reviewers not liking the graphics. Everyone else agreed.

Stephano pointed out that before the company merger, designers had worked closely with authors but now worked separately. He speculated that many of the graphics needed rework because the authors didn't explain to the designers what information the graphics were meant to convey.

Jeremy suggested that they use a diagram to show other managers how the team traced the root cause to the problem.

Logic Diagram

Because authors don't convey design ideas well and **because** designers enter the process after text is finalized:

| Designers are not sure what is expected for design concepts | **and** | Designers get little direction on creating graphics |

So
Book reviewers don't like the graphics

and

Because graphics are too sketchy and are not well integrated with text

Rework and project delays result

5. **Verify the root cause(s).**
   - If possible and practical, conduct a test under controlled conditions (Design of Experiments) to determine the effects of changes to the suspected root cause(s), or to cause the problem to appear in otherwise stable processes.

How can I turbo-charge this step?
Weighted Criteria Decision Matrix

There will be some situations where teams don't have enough data to help them reach a conclusion on the root cause(s) of the problem. In these situations, teams can use a Decision Matrix to reach consensus on the most likely root cause(s). This tool helps a team compare the leading candidates for the root cause against criteria that the team decides are important for selecting a root cause. Use the following steps to construct a Decision Matrix.

1. Weight each criterion on a scale of 1–9, with "1" indicating a low value and "9" indicating a high value. Make sure each criterion has a different weight.

   - Your team's criteria may change depending on the problem. Some examples of criteria include:

   – Creates exciting quality for the customer.

   – Can be implemented quickly.

   – Creates a positive change.

   – Cost is minimal or within budget.

   – Minimal resistance to changing the root cause.

---

2. Rate each possible root cause against each criterion. An example of a rating system the team may use:

9 = Strongly meets the criterion

5 = Moderately meets the criterion

1 = Weakly meets the criterion

Place the team's ratings in the top left portion of each "cell" in the matrix.
3. Multiply each rating by the weight of the criterion and place this number in the bottom-right portion of each cell.
4. Tally the scores and select the root cause with the highest score.

Weighted Criteria
Decision Matrix

Notice that root cause #1 has the highest score. The team would address this root cause.

Criteria	Weight	Root Causes		
		1	2	3
1. Creates exciting quality for the customer	9	9 / 81	5 / 45	5 / 45
2. Can be implemented quickly	7	9 / 63	5 / 35	1 / 7
3. Creates a positive change	5	1 / 5	0 / 0	5 / 25
	Totals	149	80	77

Interrelationship Digraph (*MJII*, p. 76.)

The Interrelationship Digraph (ID) is an excellent tool to use when there is a high degree of uncertainty in the problem and there is little or no historical data available to guide the team. The ID, which shows the cause and effect relationships among possible causes of an outcome, allows a team to identify the key drivers of a desired outcome.

Use the following steps to construct an ID.

1. Agree on the desired goal, objective, or outcome and phrase it as a question.

2. Use separate Post-it™ Notes or cards to list the team's ideas on what could cause or influence the outcome. Use large, bold printing, including a large number or letter on each idea for quick reference. Keep the number of ideas manageable, between 5 and 25.

3. Arrange the cards or notes in a large circle. Leave enough space so that the team can draw lines between the ideas.

4. Look for cause/influence relationships between all of the ideas and draw relationship arrows.

   • Choose any of the ideas as a starting point. When a relationship exists between two ideas, draw a relationship arrow from the one that causes or influences the other.

5. Tally the number of outgoing and incoming arrows for each idea. Write the tally for outgoing and incoming arrows next to each idea.

   • Find the idea with the highest number of outgoing arrows and label it as the "Driver."

   • Find the idea with the highest number of incoming arrows and label it as the "Outcome."

Interrelationship Digraph

What are the issues related to reducing litter?

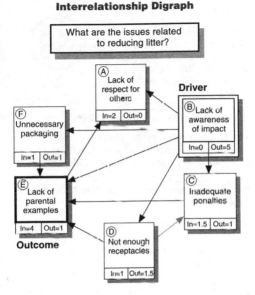

Reproduced from the MJII, p. 80.

Step 4

Develop a Solution and Action Plan:

Develop an effective solution and action plan, including targets for improvement.

What does this step do?

Helps teams develop practical solutions and an action plan to effectively address the root cause(s) of a problem, and produce a desired effect or outcome.

What concepts must I understand to do this step?

Finding New Approaches Can Require Innovative Thinking

People interpret information and situations based on past experience. This helps them to build on existing knowledge of what works. However, these experiences can also trap people into automatically using methods that worked in the past when the current situation requires innovative thinking. To prevent this from happening, teams can ask:

- Has the situation happened before?
- What did the team and/or organization do?
- What were the results?
- How is it different this time?
- What could be done differently to get better results?
- What are alternative ways of solving the problem?

Benefits of an Action Plan

The plan should describe expected results, tasks that need to be accomplished, start and end times for tasks, names of individuals who are responsible for completing assigned tasks, an assessment of the risks, and estimates of costs and staff resources. The benefits of an action plan are:

- Good communications within the team and among stakeholders.
- Focused energy.
- The team has a baseline for measuring effectiveness.
- People know what is expected of them and can perform better with this knowledge.
- Teams have a method for evaluating alternatives against important criteria, sequencing tasks, and estimating resources (such as time, costs, and staffing needs.)

Importance of Assessing Risks and Building Countermeasures into the Plan

When teams implement a new process or make a major modification to a process, there is always a degree of risk. One way to reduce the risk is to identify areas where something could go wrong during implementation (a contingency), and then plan countermeasures to put in place if the contingency becomes real.

What actions must be taken in this step?
- **Generate** potential **solutions**.
- **Select** the most effective **solution**.
- **Generate all possible tasks** that can be done to implement the solution.

- Anticipate likely problems (contingencies) and develop possible **countermeasures**.
- Create an **action plan**.

How do I do it? 🏃

1. **Generate potential solutions.**
   - In preparation for this step, make sure that your team includes the people who are most familiar with the problem or process, as well as customers of the process.
   - Write down the root cause(s) of the problem so that the team can refer to it (them) while composing the solution statement(s).

   a) Write one or more solution statements for each root cause.
   - There are three components of an effective solution statement: 1) the action the implementation team will take; 2) what or whom the action will involve; and 3) what the desired effect will be.

What action will you take?	+	To what? Or with whom?	+	To produce what desired effect?
Replace	+	spark plugs	+	to increase fuel economy
Improve training	+	for all employees	+	to reduce turnover
Provide recommended maintenance	+	on photocopiers	+	to reduce paper waste caused by jams

b) Other methods for generating potential solutions are Classic Brainstorming (*MJII*, p. 19 or *CTMJ*, p. 31) and Imaginary Brainstorming (*CTMJ*, p. 39).

- If the results from Classic Brainstorming are inadequate, try using Imaginary Brainstorming to stretch each team member's thinking.
- If the team has a list of ideas that were generated by Classic Brainstorming, hold onto it. Classic Brainstorming is the first step in the Imaginary Brainstorming process.

ABC Team
Composes a Solution Statement

When team members reviewed the Cause & Effect Diagram, they all agreed that the delays in product development were caused by the graphic designers and authors not consulting with one another. Consequently, the graphics were unacceptable and had to be reworked most of the time. The team composed the following solution statement:

What action will you take?		To what? Or with whom?		To produce what desired effect?
Change	+	the authoring and graphics production phases	+	to reduce graphics rework and to complete projects as scheduled

2. **Rank potential solutions; select the best solution.**

   a) Identify the selection criteria that will be used to rank the solutions.

   - Identify the most important customer needs. These needs should always be the team's first consideration for defining criteria for selecting a solution. Any solution that fails the "customer test" should not go any further in the problem-solving process.

   - Agree on the additional criteria that will be used by the team to assess all of the potential solutions. Typical criteria include:
     - Level of complexity
     - Level of resources required
     - Amount of time required for implementation
     - Degree of control by the team
     - Probability of change
     - Impact on the problem (high, medium, low)

   > Limit the number of criteria to a maximum of three or four. Evaluating the solutions against too many criteria can become a complex and tiresome process.

   b) Use a Matrix Diagram (*MJII*, p. 85), Weighted Criteria Decision Matrix (p. 58 in this book), or the Prioritization Matrices tool (*MJII*, p. 105) to select the best solution.

   - Plot the solutions against the criteria.
   - Unless there are significant disagreements among team members, the criteria can be used as if they are all equally important.

Matrix Diagram Example

Criteria / Solutions	Criterion 1	Criterion 2	Criterion 3
Solution 1	High	Medium	Low
Solution 2	High	High	High
Solution 3	Low	High	Medium
Solution 4	Low	Medium	Medium

High = Strongly meets criterion
Medium = Moderately meets criterion
Low = Weakly meets criterion

> ✔ When ranking the solutions, limit the number of solutions to no more than eight. If the team has more than eight, narrow down the list by consensus or a ranking method such as Multivoting or Nominal Group Technique (*MJII*, p 91).

- If the criteria are not equally important, use a Weighted Criteria Matrix or the Prioritization Matrices tool (*MJII*, p. 105).
- When teams use the Full Analytical Criteria Method for the Prioritization Matrices tool, it forces a discussion of assumptions right from the beginning of the comparison of criteria. Each step of the process gives team members a chance to understand why people may agree or disagree over the relative importance of the criteria.

- Remember that team members often rank several different solutions very highly. The team should feel free to choose one from the top two or three highest ranked solutions without agonizing over the math. In fact, sometimes for the best results, the team should pursue more than one solution at a time.

The following example is a simple illustration of the Full Analytical Criteria Method for constructing the Prioritization Matrices. (For more detailed examples, see the Coach's Guide to The Memory Jogger™ II, *pp. 150–153 or* The Memory Jogger Plus+®, *pp. 99–134.)*

Prioritization Matrices Example: Improving the Lead Time for Restocking Books in Inventory

Criterion vs. Criterion Matrix
Weighting the Criteria

Criteria	Cost to implement	Quick to implement	Acceptable by employees	Level of training needed	Impact on other departments	Row Total (5 criteria)	Relative Decimal Value (Divide Row Total by Grand Total)
Cost to implement		1/10	1/5	1/5	1/10	.60	.01
Quick to implement	10		5	1	5	21	.36
Acceptable by employees	5	1/5		1/5	1/5	5.6	.10
Level of training needed	5	1	5		5	16	.27
Impact on other departments	10	1/5	5	1/5		15.4	.26

Weighted Scale
- 1 = Equally important
- 5 = More important
- 10 = Much more important
- 1/5 = Less important
- 1/10 = Much less important

Grand Total (5 criteria)	58.6

> ☑ For each weight (e.g., 1, 5, 10) recorded in a row cell, also record its reciprocal value (e.g., 1/5, 1/10) in the corresponding column cell.

> ☑ Before adding together the scores, convert the 1/5 and 1/10 fractions to decimal values, e.g., 1/5 = .20 and 1/10 = .10.

Solutions vs. Each Criterion Matrix
(Cost Criterion)

Cost to implement	Solution 1	Solution 2	Solution 3	Solution 4	Solution 5	Row Total	Relative Decimal Value (Divide Row Total by Grand Total)
Solution 1		5	1/10	1/10	1/5	5.4	.09
Solution 2	1/5		5	10	5	20.2	.32
Solution 3	10	1/5		1	5	16.2	.26
Solution 4	10	1/10	1		1/5	11.3	.18
Solution 5	5	1/5	1/5	5		10.2	.16

Weighted Scale
1 = Equal cost
5 = Less expensive
10 = Much less expensive
1/5 = More expensive
1/10 = Much more expensive

Grand Total 63.3

- For each criterion, create an L-shaped matrix with all of the solutions on both the vertical and horizontal axis and the criteria listed in the left-hand corner of the matrix. *There will be as many solutions matrices as there are criteria to be applied.*

Prioritization Matrices Example, continued

Solutions vs. Each Criterion Matrix
(Quick to Implement Criterion)

Quick to implement	Solution 1	Solution 2	Solution 3	Solution 4	Solution 5	Row Total	Relative Decimal Value (Divide Row Total by Grand Total)
Solution 1		10	5	5	5	25	.45
Solution 2	1/10		1	5	10	16.1	.29
Solution 3	1/5	1		5	5	11.2	.20
Solution 4	1/5	1/5	1/5		1	1.6	.03
Solution 5	1/5	1/10	1/5	1		1.5	.03

Weighted Scale Grand Total 55.4

1 = Equal amount of time to implement
5 = Less time to implement
10 = Much less time to implement
1/5 = More time to implement
1/10 = Much more time to implement

Use the same scale you used for comparing each criterion against one another, 1, 5, 10, etc., but customize the wording for each criterion. Note that 5 and 10 weights are always used for the positive or desirable condition, and the reciprocals 1/5 and 1/10 used for the negative or undesirable condition. For example: with the criterion "cost to implement," it is usually desirable if implementation is "less expensive," (a weight of 5). With the criterion "acceptable by employees," it is usually desirable to implement a solution that is "more acceptable by employees," (also a weight of 5).

© 2000 GOAL/QPC

Solutions vs. Each Criterion Matrix
(Acceptable by Employees Criterion)

Acceptable by employees	Solution 1	Solution 2	Solution 3	Solution 4	Solution 5	Row Total	Relative Decimal Value (Divide Row Total by Grand Total)
Solution 1		1/5	1/5	1/10	1/10	.60	0
Solution 2	5		1/5	1/5	1/10	5.3	.08
Solution 3	5	5		1/5	1/5	10.2	.15
Solution 4	10	5	5		1/5	20.2	.30
Solution 5	10	10	5	5		30	.45

Weighted Scale
1 = Equally acceptable
5 = Less acceptable
10 = Much less acceptable
1/5 = More acceptable
1/10 = Much more acceptable

Grand Total 66.3

Solutions vs. Each Criterion Matrix
(Level of Training Needed Criterion)

Level of training needed	Solution 1	Solution 2	Solution 3	Solution 4	Solution 5	Row Total	Relative Decimal Value (Divide Row Total by Grand Total)
Solution 1		1	5	1/5	5	11.2	.20
Solution 2	1		5	1	10	17	.31
Solution 3	1/5	1/5		1/10	5	5.5	.10
Solution 4	5	1	10		5	21	.38
Solution 5	1/5	1/10	1/5	1/5		.70	.01

Weighted Scale
1 = Equal training needed
5 = Less training needed
10 = Much less training needed
1/5 = More training needed
1/10 = Much more training needed

Grand Total 55.4

Prioritization Matrices Example, continued

Solutions vs. Each Criterion Matrix
(Impact on Other Departments Criterion)

Impact on other departments	Solution 1	Solution 2	Solution 3	Solution 4	Solution 5	Row Total	Relative Decimal Value (Divide Row Total by Grand Total)
Solution 1		5	5	1	10	21	.37
Solution 2	1/5		1	5	10	16.2	.28
Solution 3	1/5	1		5	10	16.2	.28
Solution 4	1	1/5	1/5		1	2.2	.04
Solution 5	1/10	1/10	1/10	1		1.3	.02

Weighted Scale
1 = Equal impact
5 = Less impact
10 = Much less impact
1/5 = More impact
1/10 = Much more impact

Grand Total: 56.9

- Use the weighted criteria matrix (see p. 68) to transfer the relative decimal values to each criterion in the summary matrix.

- Using one "solutions vs. each criterion" matrix at a time (pp. 69–72), transfer the relative decimal values for each solution to the corresponding criterion column in the summary matrix.

- Multiply the two numbers in each cell to get a score for each cell in the row; add the scores to get a row total for each solution; and lastly, figure out the relative decimal values for each solution.

© 2000 GOAL/QPC

Summary Matrix
Solutions vs. All Criteria

Criteria / Solutions	Cost to implement (.01)	Quick to implement (.36)	Acceptable by employees (.10)	Level of training needed (.27)	Impact on other departments (.26)	Row Total	Relative Decimal Value (Divide Row Total by Grand Total)
Solution 1	.01 x .09 = 0	.36 x .45 = .16	.10 x 0 = 0	.27 x .20 = .05	.26 x .37 = .14	.35	.35
Solution 2	.01 x .32 = 0	.36 x .29 = .10	.10 x .08 = .01	.27 x .31 = .08	.26 x .28 = .07	.26	.26
Solution 3	.01 x .26 = 0	.36 x .20 = .07	.10 x .15 = .02	.27 x .10 = .03	.26 x .28 = .07	.19	.19
Solution 4	.01 x .18 = 0	.01 x .03 = .06	.10 x .30 = .03	.27 x .38 = .03	.26 x .04 = .01	.13	.13
Solution 5	.01 x .16 = 0	.36 x .03 = .10	.10 x .45 = .05	.27 x .01 = 0	.26 x .02 = .01	.07	.07
					Grand Total	1.00	

- Compare the final decimal values to help you decide which solutions are the best ones to pursue.

3. **Generate all possible tasks that can be done to implement the solution.**
   - Use the solution statement to think about and brainstorm potential possible ways to implement the solution. (See Brainstorming in *MJII*, p. 19 or *CTMJ*, p. 31.)

ABC Team Brainstorms Tasks

The team used Classic Brainstorming to generate a list of possible tasks to reduce graphics rework.

Change standard procedures

Compare old and current process

Ask designers to review marketing research

How do other publishers run projects?

How do other industries use creative teams?

Include designers in focus groups

Change the process

Add graphics staff to the team

Provide team building training

Have designers & authors create design ideas

Decide who has final say

Create different process scenarios

Give designers & authors personality tests and match them

Study practices of award-winning publishers

Benchmark other industries

© 2000 GOAL/QPC

4. **Construct a detailed action plan.**
   - A solution is only as effective as its action plan. A good plan will document the identified tasks to implement the solution, the necessary resources, the required tasks, and the names of individuals or groups who are assigned the responsibility for completing the tasks.
   - The plan will also include milestones for assessing progress toward the team's goals or targets, as well as measures on the performance of the process. Use the table on the next page as a reference for understanding the basic elements of a good plan. (For more detailed information on developing the elements of a good plan, consult the *PMMJ*, pp. 51–134.)
   - The following sections a) through e) are a suggested tool set for teams to develop a detailed action plan.

   a) Use an Affinity Diagram to organize the team's list of potential tasks into broad groupings of tasks. (*MJII*, p. 12 for Affinity Diagram and *MJII*, p. 158 for Action Affinity.)
   - Without talking ("silent sorting"), sort the brainstormed list of cards or Post-it™ Notes into groupings that express similar themes.
   - Create summary or header cards for each grouping. The team should agree on a concise statement that best describes the grouping's central idea.

Elements of a Good Action Plan*

Element	Purpose
Define the scope (implementation of the solution)	To produce a plan that will satisfy everyone's needs. It will define the customers and what results they expect, and defines the criteria for judging the satisfaction with the results.
Complete the list of required reviews and approvals	To define the reviews and approvals that allow the team to keep on track and moving forward with everyone's approval.
Assess the risks	To understand the obstacles that could prevent the implementation of the plan.
Complete the list of required status reports	To define the reports that will be distributed to the team members, team sponsor, and customers on the progress of the project. It will highlight any problems that are occurring and what's being done to overcome them.
Review the team membership	To ensure that the team members continue to bring the right skills and expertise to the problem-solving effort. If additional skills and knowledge are required, the team will need to find and include these people on the team.
Create a schedule	To coordinate the activities efficiently to meet the deadline.
Estimate the staff effort required	To estimate the time required to make the needed resources available, and to identify activities that may interfere with other work assignments.
Create a budget	To identify costs that will be incurred to carry out the action plan.
Assemble the plan	To document the plan for final review and approval by the team, sponsor, and customers.

*The information in this table was adapted from the PMMJ, Chapter 4, "How to Create a Project Plan," pp. 51–134.

b) Use a **Tree Diagram** to map out detailed levels of tasks. (*MJII*, p. 156.)

- Use the header cards from the team's Affinity Diagram for the major headings in a Tree Diagram. These task areas are the major "sub-goals" or "means" by which the plan will be achieved.

- Break down each major task area into more detail by providing answers to the question: "What needs to be addressed to achieve the solution?" (Keep the tasks at roughly the same level of detail.) Repeat the question for each successive level until the team agrees there is enough detail to complete the plan or until the assignable tasks can be delegated.

- Review the completed Tree Diagram to determine if all the tasks need to be done. If team members are unsure about the value of some tasks, use a Decision Matrix or the Prioritization Matrices tool to evaluate the possible tasks against important criteria, such as costs, risks, timelines of completion, ease of implementation, and feasibility.

- Review the completed Tree Diagram to determine if all the necessary tasks are included. If necessary tasks were omitted, add them to the diagram.

✔ As each level of detail is developed, the team should ask, "Is there anything that we've forgotten?" before moving on to the next level.

✔ Some items may need additional levels of detail to be complete.

© 2000 GOAL/QPC   **The 7-Step Model**   77

c) Use a **Responsibility Matrix** (*MJII*, p. 85 for Matrix Diagram) to show which individuals are responsible for carrying out the key tasks in the Tree Diagram and include the time, budget, and staff allocations for each task. The team needs to address these questions:

- Who is responsible for seeing that the task is completed?
- When will the task begin?
- When will the task end?
- What is the budget for completing the task?
- What staff resources will be allocated to complete the task? (Staff days, weeks, months?)

d) Prepare a **Gantt Chart** to use as a scheduling and monitoring tool. (*MJII*, p. 9.)

- On the vertical axis, list all the tasks that must be completed.
- Across the top of the horizontal axis, list the time periods covered in the project plan. These could be days, weeks, months, quarters, years, etc.
- Indicate the starting and ending date for each task with a horizontal bar. (This information may already be available if the team has created a Responsibility Matrix.)
- Include a list of key dates below the Gantt Chart to highlight the milestones of the project.

e) Use the **Process Decision Program Chart (PDPC)** to develop countermeasures for problems that may occur during the implementation of the plan. (*MJII*, p. 160.)

- The PDPC is an ideal tool to help teams anticipate potential problems before they occur.
- Determine proposed implementation steps. These steps can be taken from the Tree Diagram.
- Develop a list of potential and likely problems (contingencies) that could interfere with the successful completion of a step by asking "What could go wrong?"
- Branch likely problems off each step.
- Branch possible and reasonable countermeasures off each likely problem.
- Choose the most effective countermeasures and build them into the plan.

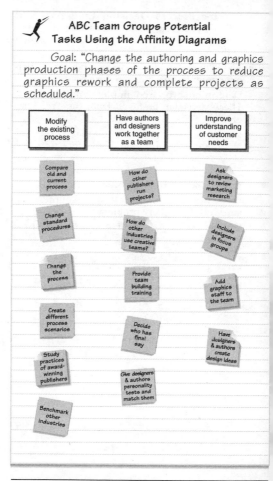

ABC Team Groups Potential Tasks Using the Affinity Diagrams

Goal: "Change the authoring and graphics production phases of the process to reduce graphics rework and complete projects as scheduled."

Modify the existing process	Have authors and designers work together as a team	Improve understanding of customer needs
Compare old and current process	How do other publishers run projects?	Ask designers to review marketing research
Change standard procedures	How do other industries use creative teams?	Include designers in focus groups
Change the process	Provide team building training	Add graphics staff to the team
Create different process scenarios	Decide who has final say	Have designers & authors create design ideas
Study practices of award-winning publishers	Give designers & authors personality tests and match them	
Benchmark other industries		

© 2000 GOAL/QPC

ABC Team Maps Out Tasks with Tree Diagram

The team used the header cards from the Affinity Diagram to create the first level of the Tree Diagram.

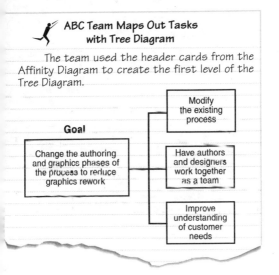

Goal

Change the authoring and graphics phases of the process to reduce graphics rework

- Modify the existing process
- Have authors and designers work together as a team
- Improve understanding of customer needs

ABC Team's Tree Diagram, continued

The team then filled in additional levels of detail by asking: "What needs to be addressed to achieve the solution?" for each successive level. Part of the team's diagram is shown below.

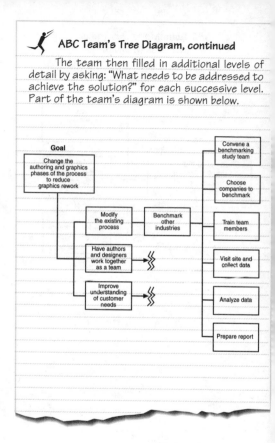

ABC Team Creates Responsibility Matrix

After completing the Tree Diagram, the team developed a Responsibility Matrix.

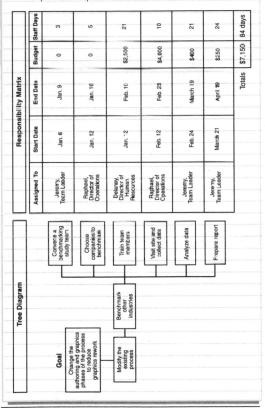

Responsibility Matrix

	Assigned To	Start Date	End Date	Budget	Staff Days
Convene a benchmarking study team	Jeremy, Team Leader	Jan. 6	Jan. 9	0	3
Choose companies to benchmark	Raphael, Director of Operations	Jan. 12	Jan. 16	0	5
Train team members	Delaney, Director of Human Resources	Jan. 2	Feb. 10	$2,500	21
Visit site and collect data	Raphael, Director of Operations	Feb. 12	Feb. 23	$4,000	10
Analyze data	Jeremy, Team Leader	Feb. 24	March 19	$400	21
Prepare report	Jeremy, Team Leader	March 21	April 19	$250	24
			Totals	$7,150	84 days

Tree Diagram

Goal: Change the authoring and graphics phases of the process to reduce graphics rework

- Benchmark other industries
  - Convene a benchmarking study team
  - Choose companies to benchmark
  - Train team members
  - Visit site and collect data
  - Analyze data
  - Prepare report
- Modify the existing process

The Gantt Chart below shows the timelines for the various activities that were planned to solve the rework problem. Jeremy, the team leader, used this chart and the Responsibility Matrix (on previous page) to prepare for a briefing with other managers.

Task	Jan.				Feb.				March				April				May			
	1	2	3	4	1	2	3	4	1	2	3	4	1	2	3	4	1	2	3	4
1. Convene a benchmarking study team	■																			
2. Choose companies to benchmark	■																			
3. Train team members		■	■																	
4. Visit site and collect data						■														
5. Analyze data										■	■									
6. Prepare report													■	■						
7. Review report with authors and designers																■				
8. Develop flow of proposed revised process																			■	

ABC Team Creates PDPC

Because ABC had never done a benchmarking study (Task 2 in the Gantt Chart), team members agreed that this was an area where they were unsure if the planned budget and time allocations were correct. The team used a PDPC to look at what factors might interfere with the successful completion of this task and selected several countermeasures to use if the problems actually occurred.

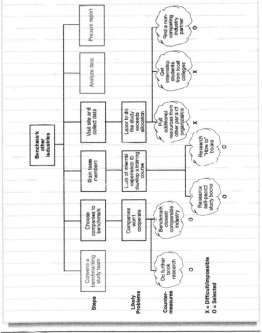

How can I turbo-charge this step?

The Activity Network Diagram (*MJII*, p. 3).

This tool allows a team to find the most efficient path and realistic schedule for the completion of a project by graphically showing total completion time, the necessary sequence of tasks, those tasks that can be done simultaneously, and the critical tasks to monitor.

1. Record all of the tasks that need to be accomplished on separate cards or Post-it™ Notes.
2. Find the first task that must be done and place it on the extreme left of a large work surface.
3. Place other tasks that can be done simultaneously above or below the first task.
4. Ask, "What is the next task that must be done?" "Can others be done simultaneously?"
5. Repeat this questioning process until all the recorded tasks are placed in sequence left to right on the page. Use parallel paths whenever possible.
6. Number each task, draw the connecting arrows, and write in the time needed to complete each task.
7. Determine the project's critical path. (Teams can either calculate the longest cumulative path or identify the tasks with no "slack" time.)
8. Determine the total time to complete the project.

Activity Network Example

Phase 1: ISO 9000 Certification Audit Schedule

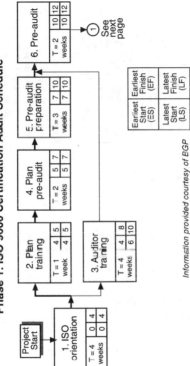

Information provided courtesy of BGP

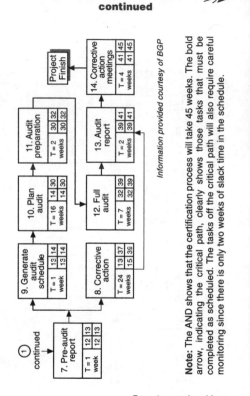

Information provided courtesy of BGP

Note: The AND shows that the certification process will take 45 weeks. The bold arrow, indicating the critical path, clearly shows those tasks that must be completed as scheduled. The tasks off the critical path will also require careful monitoring since there is only two weeks of slack time in the schedule.

Example reproduced from
The Memory Jogger™ II, *pages 10 and 11.*

Morphological Box *(CTMJ, p. 71).*

Teams may want to consider different solution scenarios to find the one that best fits their needs. The Morphological Box helps a team build these scenarios by creatively linking different options for the key parameters of the solution.

1. List the selected parameters in the left-hand column of the table.

   - A parameter is a characteristic that a solution must have to be effective.

2. Generate practical options for each parameter. Identify a minimum of two, but usually no more than five or six. More options are not always better.

   - Options are different ways that a parameter can be met.

3. Build alternative solution scenarios by linking different options.

   - Use a different symbol for each scenario. Suggestions: square, circle, oval, triangle.

   - Draw the symbols in the selected option "cells," then link similar symbols by drawing a line between them.

4. Summarize the alternative solution scenarios in narrative form.

5. Select the best solution(s).

Designing a New Process for Selecting Managers at Compass Products

Parameters	Options				
Participants	Peers	Resorts	Bosses	Internal customers	Supplier
Atmosphere	Formal	Informal			
Areas of Inquiry	Technical knowledge	Values	Decision-making style	Communications style	Teamwork style
Decision-Making Method for Selecting the Person	Consensus	Unanimity	Majority rules	Boss's choice	
Number of People Interacting	One on one	Team			
Process Documentation	Notes	Video	Audio		
Location of the Process	Facility	Corporate offices	Assessment center		

Alternative #1 ☆   Alternative #2 ⬤

Continued on next page

Analysis

The Morphological Box made it possible (theoretically) for the team to consider as many as 3600 unique models for selecting a new manager. Out of the handful that it reviewed closely, the team chose two alternatives.

In the first alternative, (the gray stars), **a team** of **internal customers** would assess each candidate's **technical knowledge** by working with him/her in a **formal atmosphere** to solve a real operational problem at the **facility**. After the team reviews the **videotape** of the sessions, a candidate would be recommended based on the **consensus** of the team.

The second alternative, (the blue circles), would include all of the candidate's **peers** holding **informal, one-on-one meetings** with the candidates at the **facility** in order to assess each candidate's fit with the core **values** of the organization. Based on each person's **notes**, the chosen candidate must be recommended **unanimously**.

Example reproduced from
The Creativity Tools Memory Jogger™ II, *pages 81 and 82.*

Step 5

Implement the Solution:

Implement the solution or process change.

What does this step do?

Helps teams to follow their action plan to solve a problem or improve a process.

What concepts must I understand to do this step?

Leadership Responsibility

- It is the team's responsibility to "sell" the benefits of the action plan to managers, associates, and others who are affected by the problem and the project.
- The team should widely communicate the action plan through briefings, newsletters, posters, and other displays. This keeps the plan highly visible, and keeps others in the organization informed about the team's progress and interim accomplishments.
- Leaders have a responsibility to ensure that people have the resources they need to implement the action plan.

Accountability

- The team is accountable for completing the tasks in the action plan. To do this, the team should make one person accountable for completing each task in the plan.

© 2000 GOAL/QPC

- It is the team's job to monitor and document the progress of the plan and any discrepancies that occur during the implementation of the plan. (These discrepancies are called "variances.")
- It's important that the team schedule briefings with management to report on progress, roadblocks, and modifications to the plan.
- As each plan objective is met, inform all the team members and others in the organization who need to know.

Motivation and Morale
- Leaders need to remove any barriers that may impede the progress of implementing the plan.
- Leaders need to help team members stay focused and motivated, and feel supported and rewarded as they "work the plan." This is especially important during the early stages of implementation, where misunderstandings and conflicts among team members are likely to occur.
- Team members should remember to give each other support and understanding during stressful times of the implementation.

What actions must be taken in this step?
- **Practice good communication** skills.
- **Develop** good team **meeting skills.**
- **Analyze data** to determine what changes are needed, if any, and to **document** the team's **ongoing assessment of the plan.**
- **Make effective and timely decisions** based on data, not hunches, whenever possible.

How do I do it? 🏃

1. **Communicate the plan.**
   - Get the plan approved.
   - All team members should understand their roles and responsibilities in carrying out the planned activities and should know the details of the plan, including milestones and what reports will be required.
   - Explain the plan to people who will be affected by the plan's activities. This will help people understand the full scope of the plan, see where and how they will be affected by the plan, and to "buy in" to the benefits of the plan. Consider addressing these questions:
     1. What activities are planned?
     2. What will the implementation cost?
     3. What staff resources are needed?
     4. When will the implementation of the plan be completed?
     5. What are the benefits of carrying out the plan?

ABC Team Discusses the Plan

After the team developed an action plan (Step 4), the team scheduled a meeting and briefed Hanna Gibbons, the project sponsor, on the following information:

- The tasks/activities in the plan.
- The budget to implement the plan.
- Staff requirements.
- Projected beginning and ending dates for implementing the plan.
- The benefits of the plan.

During the briefing, Hanna suggested a less expensive and less time-consuming way of conducting the benchmarking study, and indicated that she wanted a weekly briefing on the team's progress.

2. **Carry out and monitor the implementation.**
   - Carry out the action steps to achieve interim and final objectives of the plan.
   - Monitor the time spent on the project and the resources used to ensure that the schedule, budget, and resources stay within the limits established in the plan.
   - Measure the performance of the implemented solution against the plan.
     - Name one person to be responsible for recording and reporting the actual performance of the solution against the plan.
     - Modify the plan and get approval, as needed.

- Implement any countermeasures when anticipated obstacles actually occur. See page 77 for a description of how the Process Decision Program Chart is used in planning countermeasures.

- Document the changes.

✦ ABC Team Implements the Plan

As the benchmarking team members began the detailed planning for their site visit, they soon recognized that the resources assigned would be inadequate to complete the tasks during the allotted timeframe.

Extending the timeframe would delay the data analysis to such an extent that the completion schedule would be delayed.

The team recommended implementing the planned countermeasure for this problem, i.e., "find a non-competing industry partner." Since the industry partner had already been identified and contacted, the team scheduled a meeting to identify roles and finalize the details of the joint site effort.

© 2000 GOAL/QPC

Task	Assigned To	Start Date	Planned End Date	Actual End Date	Corrective Action(s) Taken
Convene a bench-marking study group	Jeremy, Team Leader	Jan. 6	Jan. 9	Jan. 9	None
Choose companies to benchmark	Raphael, Director of Operations	Jan. 12	Jan. 16	Jan. 16	None
Train team members	Delaney, Director of Human Resources	Jan. 12	Feb. 10	Mar. 1	None
Visit site and collect data	Raphael, Director of Operations	Feb. 12	Feb. 23	Mar. 5*	Contacted non-competing business partner to participate in the site visit.

*Explanation: The ABC team's resources are not adequate to complete the site visit and to collect benchmarking data within the time allotted.

ABC Team Implements
the Plan, continued

The team also scheduled lunch hour briefings to keep other employees informed about the progress of the implementation.

The team used the results of the benchmarking study to conclude they needed to create a space just for designers and authors to meet and discuss design concepts.

In the revised process, authors and designers used the "design concept room" to create three different designs for book graphics. These designs were included with the book draft sent to the book reviewers.

3. **Meet regularly to share information on the implementation.**
   - Have regularly scheduled review meetings to inform managers and others about progress, delays, and needed adjustments.
     - Create agendas for meetings.
     - Develop and maintain effective team meeting skills, which include listening, giving and receiving feedback, adhering to the team's ground rules, and learning how to handle conflicts between team members.
   - Issue status reports.
     - Determine who should receive them.
     - Create a checklist of what information should be included in each report.

– Report on discrepancies (variances) and the team's corrective actions, if any.

- Keep everyone informed about the implementation of the plan by using a well publicized and highly visible storyboard or write regular updates for the company newsletter or Intranet site. (See Chapter 4, p. 121 to learn more about storyboards.)

The team's documentation of variances from the plan and/or implemented corrective actions/countermeasures can provide valuable input for the team's later review of "things that helped" and "things to avoid" in the future.

ABC Team Reports on Progress of the Plan

Team members met regularly to discuss progress on the implementation. To keep others in the organization informed on the implementation, the team:

- Wrote an article for the company newsletter explaining the goals of the improvement plan and the key events and dates.
- Updated the storyboard to track the progress of the implementation plan.
- Conducted a briefing to explain the revised process and "design concept room" to other employees.

How can I turbo-charge this step?

Use project-planning software to track the performance of the implemented solution against the plan. This will enable the team to see if the project is running ahead of or behind schedule, and if it is on target with the allotted resources, i.e., money and labor. Many of the graphic capabilities of the software can also be used for briefings and to update the team's storyboard.

Step 6

Review and Evaluate:
*Review and evaluate
the results of the change.*

Plan

Act

Do

Check

What does this step do?

Helps teams assess the results of the change and evaluate whether the change met the team's objectives.

What concepts must I understand to do this step?

The Power of the Plan-Do-Check-Act (PDCA) Model

When teams use a systematic approach to problem solving, problems are solved more efficiently, teams' efforts are focused and directed, and the results gain greater credibility with management and with their customers.

The Power of the Standardize-Do-Check-Act (SDCA) Model

When the changes that teams make are the right ones, teams should *standardize* them. This sub-cycle of the PDCA model ensures that process improvements are made permanent.

Learn from Experience

When teams take the time to review and evaluate the processes they used to solve a problem, the organization can learn from the teams' experiences. This review can help others to be more efficient and effective in the future.

What actions must be taken in this step?

- **Understand** the importance and role of process and outcome **measures**.
- Know how to **interpret** a **Run Chart** and **Pareto Chart**.
- **Create** and maintain **procedures, documents, and records**.
- **Communicate** process **changes**.

How do I do it? 🏃

1. **Review the results of the change.**

   - Is there a difference between present and past performance?

   - What are the team's success measures? Did the team meet its targets? If yes, continue to implement the plan. If no, find out why.

   - Did the solution work? If not, try any of the following:

     - Examine the team's thinking process that led to the chosen solution.

     - Use a Check Sheet, Pareto Chart, Run Chart, Control Chart, or Histogram to check the results of the change and to compare prior performance with current performance. (To determine which one of these tools is most appropriate, consult the table on page 54.)

     - If new issues have surfaced as a result of the change made, use the Affinity Diagram to categorize them. (*MJII*, p. 12.)

     - To confirm whether the team's solution to the problem was the best choice, create a new Pareto Chart that relates to the new Flowchart of the process. Look for a relationship between

---

the changes made in the sub-step measures
and the overall process measures to confirm
the solution.

- Review, refine, or redo the Cause and Effect
  Diagram to see if the team can identify another
  root cause.

- Develop an alternative solution.

• Modify the process to prevent a recurrence.

> ✔ Whatever tools were used in Step 3 to vali-
> date the root cause, before the change was
> made, should also be used after the change is
> made.

> ✔ Changes made to increase the speed of a
> process may not produce the desired results
> until all people working in the process are
> familiar with the new steps.

ABC Team Discusses
How to Evaluate the Results

After using the revised process for the next book project, the team compared these results against the data for previous projects to determine if the change was an improvement.

To evaluate the results, the team wanted to know:

- Is the process substantially changed? Do managers and associates perceive the change as an improvement?
- Is there a reduction in the number of graphics that needed to be reworked after the second book review? What is the extent of the reduction?
- Are projects completed on time?
- Do authors and graphic designers work well as a team?
- Is employee morale improving?
- Are there any unanticipated benefits or negative consequences?

With the newest book project, only six of the 45 graphics needed rework after the second book review and the project was completed two days ahead of schedule. This was a substantial improvement!

2. Revise the process as necessary.

- Use the information the team has gathered so far to fine-tune the process.
- Brainstorm countermeasures for problems as they surface. Then revise the team's process Flowchart as necessary. Keep revising the process until the team is satisfied that the problem has been solved.
- The team may decide to establish new measures for monitoring the process.

> ✔ When the process is working well, the team might consider reducing the frequency of measures. This can lead to cost savings.

3. Standardize the improvement.

a) Get the change approved. The steps necessary to standardize a change depend on the requirements of your organization.

- Many organizations require formal approval from management, customers, or regulators (or all three) before an improvement can become a part of the standard process.
- The time a team invests to confirm and document the root cause of the problem will give the team's efforts important credibility and speed the standardization of the solution.

b) Communicate the following information to all the people affected by the change:

- The process (and its name)
- The problem
- The root cause(s) of the problem
- The solution(s) to the problem

- What each person must do differently (and the same) to remove the root cause(s)
- Written instructions, directives, and memos about the change
- The new measures that have been put into place to monitor the process
- It is important to communicate the changes to the right people. Include suppliers and customers, as well as other people who work in the process. Also, don't forget about communicating improvements to other functional areas.
- Identify the ways that information is shared in your organization. Your team may have to communicate the changes in formal training sessions, or by sharing information informally with co-workers. Written instructions, directives, and memos may also be needed as a permanent record of the change.

Don't leave people in the dark. It is better to broadcast the change than to overlook people who need to know about it. Many people not directly involved in the process may have had to compensate for the problem in the past. They'll be glad to know about the change.

c) Update documentation to reflect the changes in the process.
- Key questions a team might address:
  - Do we need a new policy or procedures?
  - Do we need a new documentation or data collection form?

© 2000 GOAL/QPC

- Who has the responsibility for updating the documentation?

- Who has the responsibility for carrying out policy and procedures?

- Useful tools for updating documentation include:

  - Tree Diagram to assign tasks to be accomplished, the person or position responsible (*PMMJ*, p. 64 and *MJII*, p. 156)

  - Flowchart for defining processes (*MJ9000/2000*, pp. 23-25, 27-28 and *MJII*, p. 56)

  - Variance calculation sheet to record deviations from important measures (*PMMJ*, p. 138)

d) Update and conduct training.

- Key questions the team might address:

  - Does training for carrying out the newly established policy and procedures, and writing documentation exist? If not, create it and train people how to do it.

  - Who will be responsible for updating or creating training?

  - Who will deliver the training?

  - Who will be trained?

  - What proficiency levels are required? How will proficiency be tested?

- The team should make presentations to management, steering teams, or other staff as required. Use the table on the next page as a guide in preparing the team's presentation.

Areas to Address in Presenting Your Results

Your Audience	• What information is important to them? • What do they already know? • What do they need to learn from the presentation and from future training? • Tell them the purpose and goals of the plan.
The Tools You Used	• Explain your team's problem-solving journey, including the process (See Chapter 4, "Creating a Storyboard.") • Point out which tools the team used, and which ones were effective.
The Status of the Project	If the problem-solving process is not complete, answer these questions: • What have you done/accomplished so far? • What do you have left to do? • What obstacles have you encountered? • Do you have any preliminary recommendations?
Your Team	• What have team members learned about themselves and other team members? • What have team members learned about their work, the organization, and the organization's suppliers and customers?
Manage the Presentation	• Who will participate in the presentation? Try to include as many team members as is feasible. • Distribute a typed report, including handouts of supporting documentation. • Reserve and know how to use the audiovisual equipment needed for the presentation.

☑ Overhead slides or a computerized presentation can help focus your audience's attention on the important points of the presentation.

☑ Large amounts of data are best presented in graphs or tables. A detailed explanation of your problem-solving process and conclusions are best presented in a written handout that members of your audience can save for future reference.

✕ ABC Team Standardizes the Improvement

Based on the results of the test of the revised process, team members felt they had implemented an effective, lasting solution to the problem of too many reworked graphics.

The team finalized the new process Flowchart, documented the standard operating procedures for the revised process, and put both the Flowchart and operating procedures on the company Intranet so that anyone could easily refer to them.

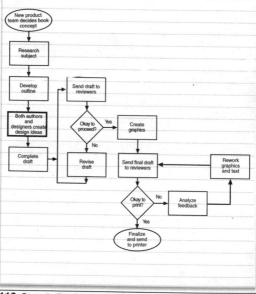

© 2000 GOAL/QPC

4. Continue to monitor the process for changes.

Designate a process champion. This is someone who has the ongoing responsibility for monitoring process measures and reporting changes to the organization. This person should be knowledgeable about the process, its documentation, procedures, and required training.

- Use the appropriate tools to monitor the process. (See Step 3, page 54 for a list of tools.)
- Establish a monitoring plan for collecting data. Address these issues:
  - How much data should be collected?
  - Who will collect it?
  - How often should it be collected?
  - What records will be kept? By whom?

ABC Team
Monitors the Change

The ABC team submitted its final report to the management group. This report contained a recommendation for appointing someone from management to be responsible for monitoring key performance areas to ensure that ABC was able to "hold the gain" in the new product development process and to identify other possible ways of improving the process in the future.

The team recommended that the reviews focus on the following:

- Feedback from the book reviewers on the quality of the graphics
- The number of unacceptable graphics
- The frequency and duration of delays caused by reworking unacceptable graphics

Jeremy accepted responsibility for tracking and reporting these measures at monthly management meetings.

How can I turbo-charge this step? ⚡➤

Teams should consider using these tools to help the organization, customers, and suppliers to more thoroughly understand the solution and how the change(s) will affect them.

- Use computers and Intranets for instantly communicating information.
- Use Force Field Analysis to identify the driving and restraining forces that will influence the required process change(s). (See *MJII*, p. 63.) Work on strengthening the driving forces and/or removing the restraining forces.
- Use the Affinity Diagram and the Interrelationship Digraph to organize the data and focus on the important issue(s) affecting the change. (See *MJII*, pp. 12 and 76, respectively.)
- Use the ISO 9000 Standards as a formal or informal process to standardize your processes and documentation. (See *MJ9000/2000*, pp. 19-40.)

Step 7

Reflect and Act on Learnings:
Learning from and improving your team's problem-solving process.

What does this step do?

Helps teams address the lessons learned from the problem-solving process and identify the next improvement opportunities.

What concepts must I understand to do this step?

Learning Organization

In a learning organization, knowledge is defined, documented, reviewed, updated, and easily available to everyone in the organization.

- The knowledge that team members and leaders have gained about what worked, what didn't work, and what needs to be done next (if anything), should be clearly understood and documented.
- When teams share their results, it helps reinforce what they learned and helps others in the organization to benefit from the team's experience so that future problem-solving efforts and team performance can be improved.

Human Dynamics and Team Spirit

To have good teams and good teamwork, team members need to:

- Continually build on their knowledge and skills.
- Build and manage cooperative relationships with others.

© 2000 GOAL/QPC

- Develop their skills in identifying and solving problems.
- Do what they can to create environments and processes that encourage people to excel in their work.

What actions must be taken in this step?
- Use Classic **Brainstorming**
- Construct and interpret the **Radar Chart**
- **Celebrate!**

How do I do it? 🏃

1. **Assess the problem-solving process the team used and the results achieved. Recommend changes, if needed.**
   - When teams make reflection and assessment part of the regular problem-solving process, they can avoid making costly mistakes in the future and can develop more productive ways of working.
   - Pay special attention to the processes that produced the results, not just the results.
     - How well did the problem get solved? How could it be better next time?
     - How well did the *process* for solving the problem work? How could it be better next time?
   - Assess the team's effectiveness on each part of the PDCA Cycle:
     - **Plan:** What did the team plan to do?
     - **Do:** What did the team actually do?
     - **Check:** What did the team find when they checked?
     - **Act:** What will be done about the differences?

- Assess the training, if training was provided as part of the team's problem-solving process.
  - What areas need improvement (tools, process, teaming, etc.)?
  - What new areas need to be covered?

- Brainstorm a list of lessons learned. What did you learn about:
  - Yourself as an individual?
  - Yourself as a team player?
  - Your customers?
  - Your organization?

☑ To assess the team's effectiveness or the team's processes, consider using the Radar Chart (*MJII*, p. 137.) This tool allows a team to assess multiple performance areas and quickly illustrates to the team what's going well, what needs improvement, and if there are gaps in team members' perceptions.

© 2000 GOAL/QPC

ABC Team Evaluates the Experience

The ABC team had a final meeting to conduct a self-assessment on how it performed as a team and to identify areas that needed to be addressed in the future by other problem-solving teams.

The team used a Radar Chart to assess five areas of performance, on a scale of 0–10, with 0 equal to "non-functioning" and 10 equal to "excellent." Individual team member scores for the five areas of performance are illustrated in the chart below.

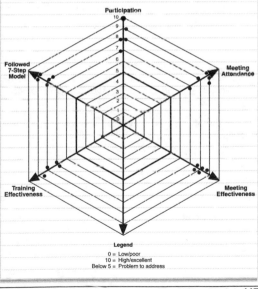

Legend
0 = Low/poor
10 = High/excellent
Below 5 = Problem to address

The team looked for clustered scores to see where members were in agreement and for extreme scores (high and low) to understand why members were not in agreement. The lowest score was a "2" for "Training Effectiveness," while the other scores for that category were "7" or higher. Stephano, who assigned the "2," explained that he rated it so low because he already knew the subject matter fairly well and didn't need the training. After the training was over, he admitted to himself that he could have probably helped the team more by using that time to do research or other work.

In light of this, the team made a recommendation to Delaney, the Director of Human Resources, to improve the department's process for determining training needs by providing staff with more detailed information about course objectives and content.

The highest score of "10" was given to "Participation," while the other scores for that category ranged only as low as "7." Lani, who assigned the "10," said that in the past she had worked almost exclusively by herself and this was a refreshing change that resulted in one of the best work experiences that she had in years.

Team members congratulated themselves for having only one score below "5," which they used as a cut-off point to indicate a serious problem or area needing attention.

2. **Continue the improvement process where needed; standardize where possible.**
   - Continue talking with customers.
   - Seek other opportunities for improvement. Consider reviewing the team's Pareto Chart (from Step 1) to select the next problem area to focus on.
   - Consider new problems that were identified during the problem-solving process but were put on a "to do" list (or "parking lot"). These problems may have been put in the parking lot because they:
     - Did not relate to the problem being addressed.
     - Were beyond the scope or capability of the team. If this is true, charter a new team to address the problem or refer the problem to management or an improvement steering team.

3. **Celebrate success.**
   - Celebrate the contribution of team members and everyone else inside or outside of the organization that supported the team's efforts. It helps to reinforce the positive feelings that come from working together to solve problems.
   - There are many ways to celebrate: Hold a party...go out to lunch...say "thank you"... present a small gift...recognize participants' successes in front of their peers. However your team chooses to celebrate, make sure it will be enjoyable for everyone.

✗ ABC Team Celebrates

The ABC team celebrated by hosting a luncheon. Team members, the project sponsor, the company president, key suppliers and customers, and a photographer were invited. Each team member received a gift desk set embossed with the project name and start and end dates.

How can I turbo-charge this step? ⚡➡

- Use the Intranet to post the team's learnings. This communication will contribute to the maintenance of a learning organization.
- Recognize and reward people for their work.

Chapter Four

Creating a Storyboard

What does a storyboard do? 🏊•

A storyboard is a self-explanatory, graphic summary of the key analyses, decisions, and actions of the problem-solving process. It keeps the organization informed of the team's progress during the Plan, Do, Check, and Act steps.

What concepts must I understand to create a storyboard?

- How the team's problem-solving effort addresses a customer-related problem.
- The team's purpose and objectives (the problem statement).
- How the team used the tools, and what actions were taken to address the problem.
- Who was involved in the problem-solving process.
- What data were collected, and how the team interpreted the data.
- The proposed solution.
- The targets, milestones, and results of the project.

What actions need to be taken to create an effective storyboard?

- **Summarize** the team's **activities and results** so that the storyboard text is simple, clear, and interesting to non-team members.
- **Create graphs and charts** that are accurate and easy to understand.

- **Present information** for quick understanding using photographs, drawings, cartoons, and other graphics.
- **Organize information** to show the sequence of events and actions as they occurred during the problem-solving process.
- **Show the relevance** of the team's objectives to the organization's objectives.

How do I create a storyboard? 🏃

1. **Assemble the materials and people needed to create the storyboard.**
   - Have ready:
     - A corkboard, whiteboard, or other flat surface you can post paper on
     - Index cards or Post-it ™ Notes
     - Pushpins or tape
     - Colored markers or pens
     - Camera
     - Computer
   - Use these supplies to capture your team's ideas and results during meetings.

   ✓ The ideal storyboarding topic is a project or initiative that has a fixed timeframe, affects and involves people, improves something, e.g., a process, product, culture, technology, and shows measurable change.

   - Choose a team member to record information for the storyboard.

2. **Post the storyboard where it will be visible to everyone in the organization.**
   - Use the storyboard to chart progress and to keep others informed.
   - Display the storyboard on a commonly used bulletin board, meeting room, or other heavily used public wall space.
   - Consider using the company's Intranet to post the storyboard.

> When your team is deciding the methods for creating and displaying the storyboard, bear in mind the likely duration of the problem-solving process, the wear and tear the storyboard will receive, and the confidentiality requirements of your organization. Also consider what areas in your organization need to know about your team's efforts.

3. **Develop the storyboard.**
   - The storyboard your team creates can be developed either *during or after* the implementation of the process improvement effort.
   - Post the problem statement on the storyboard.
   - Post information about the team, such as team member names, roles, and tasks assigned.
   - Summarize the work that is completed in each step or sub-step of the problem-solving process.
     - Avoid jargon and explain technical terms.
     - Keep the graphics and text simple so that everyone in the organization can understand the storyboard.

- Highlight the results of each step. Use photographs, graphs, and data wherever possible rather than narrative.
- Clearly show any improvement in the problem area selected, and the team's and organization's measures of success.
- Mention what the team has learned about teamwork, a particular process, the organization, its suppliers, and its customers.

✓ Make the graphics easy to understand by simplifying the design of the chart (not the data). Full grids are rarely needed, and use shades of gray rather than patterned fill. Avoid the use of legends whenever possible. Instead, write labels on the graph itself.

✓ When you present your results, make sure you order the data in ways that serve your purpose. Ask "What is the trend we want to show?" This trend may not be the order in which you collected the data.

How can I turbo-charge the storyboarding process?

- Display the storyboard during meetings to focus the team on the improvement effort. Storyboards also help maintain continuity when team membership changes.
- Consider using a software package to generate and store the storyboard.

© 2000 GOAL/QPC

Handy Checklist for Creating an Effective Storyboard

Ask...	Check for Yes
Does it describe the problem?	☐ Describes the team's task and why the problem was chosen.
Does it address a customer-related problem?	☐ Shows the relevance of the team's objectives to the organization's objectives.
Is it interesting?	☐ Uses photos, graphics, cartoons, and humor, when appropriate.
Is it clear to people at all levels?	☐ Explains abbreviations and technical terms, avoids jargon, graphics and text are clear.
Does it explain what actions were taken?	☐ Shows what was done, why, when, by whom, and how. Shows the correct usage of the tools. Captures best practice.
Does it logically describe the sequence of actions taken?	☐ Follows a logical, problem-solving process.
Does it clearly show improvement in the problem areas selected?	☐ Reports on clear measures of success in relation to the team's and organization's objectives. Includes intangible improvements. Mentions what the team has learned.
Are the metrics clearly shown on the graphs?	☐ Clearly labels the x and y axes of graphs with the measures used, e.g., number of complaints, monthly sales in dollars, percent of goods returned.

Storyboard Example

The Situation

The Browning Elementary School District recently finished a four-year building project, which combined two smaller schools into one for grades K-6. Now that the space needs of its growing student population had been met, the staff and administration felt that they should address other important issues.

For the first time, the annual survey of its stakeholders showed a decrease in satisfaction. School board meetings had come to be dominated by parents and teachers unhappy with the educational programs.

The administration decided to form a team to improve the quality of the education program, and planned a follow-up survey of stakeholders. The 2nd survey revealed that although parents and students were very happy with the building and equipment, they were not happy with the existing physical education (PE) program.

Jim Hoyt, the school's physical education teacher, led the team's effort to improve the PE program.

Artwork courtesy of Sharon McCarty

Step 1. Describe the Problem

Problem Statement: There is a high percentage of children who are dissatisfied with PE class.

Reason selected: A follow-up survey revealed that dissatisfaction with the PE program was a major cause of the growing dissatisfaction with the educational program.

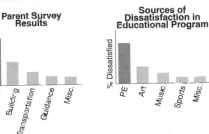

Parent Survey Results

% Dissatisfied

Quality of educational program, Building, Transportation, Guidance, Misc.

Sources of Dissatisfaction in Educational Program

% Dissatisfied

PE, Art, Music, Sports, Misc.

Team Members
1. Jim Franks, school board chairman
2. Janice Woo, principal
3. Tom Herron, staff
4. Sue Rossi, school board member
5. Albert Gupta, parent
6. Frank Smith, parent

Milestones
- Team formed. First problem statement written, distributed (9/12).
- Storyboard begun.
- Problem statement revised, distributed to team, school staff, school board (10/14).

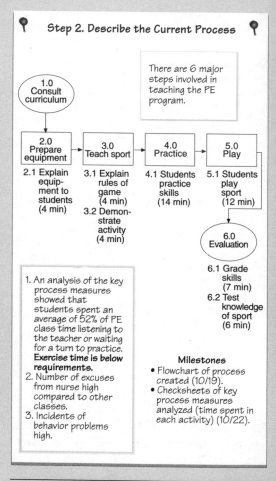

Step 2. Describe the Current Process

There are 6 major steps involved in teaching the PE program.

```
   1.0
Consult
curriculum
```

```
   2.0              3.0            4.0            5.0
 Prepare          Teach         Practice        Play
equipment         sport
```

2.1 Explain equipment to students (4 min)

3.1 Explain rules of game (4 min)
3.2 Demonstrate activity (4 min)

4.1 Students practice skills (14 min)

5.1 Students play sport (12 min)

```
   6.0
Evaluation
```

6.1 Grade skills (7 min)
6.2 Test knowledge of sport (6 min)

1. An analysis of the key process measures showed that students spent an average of 52% of PE class time listening to the teacher or waiting for a turn to practice. **Exercise time is below requirements.**
2. Number of excuses from nurse high compared to other classes.
3. Incidents of behavior problems high.

Milestones
- Flowchart of process created (10/19).
- Checksheets of key process measures analyzed (time spent in each activity) (10/22).

Step 3. Identify the Root Cause(s) of the Problem

Problem: Number of students who are dissatisfied with PE class is high.

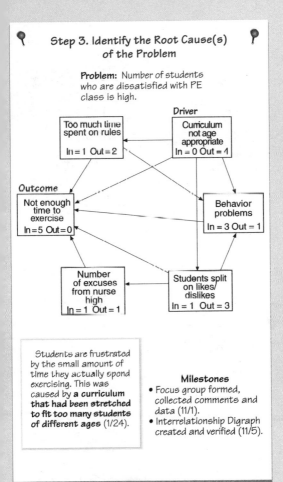

Too much time spent on rules

In = 1 Out = 2

Driver

Curriculum not age appropriate

In = 0 Out = 4

Outcome

Not enough time to exercise

In = 5 Out = 0

Behavior problems

In = 3 Out = 1

Number of excuses from nurse high

In = 1 Out = 1

Students split on likes/dislikes

In = 1 Out = 3

Students are frustrated by the small amount of time they actually spend exercising. This was caused by **a curriculum that had been stretched to fit too many students of different ages** (1/24).

Milestones
- Focus group formed, collected comments and data (11/1).
- Interrelationship Digraph created and verified (11/5).

Step 4. Develop a Solution and Action Plan

The team brainstormed possible solutions to the problem, and possible criteria to weigh the options. The option of hiring a teacher who will modify the curriculum for grades 4-6 is selected.

Criteria \ Options	Use recess time for PE	Classroom teachers teach PE	**Add new teacher**
Effectiveness (.15)	.54 x .15 (.08)	.33 x .15 (.05)	.01 x .15 (0)
Feasibility (.28)	.01 x .28 (0)	.37 x .28 (.10)	.37 x .28 (0)
Benefit to whole organization (.55)	.01 x .55 (.01)	.10 x .55 (.06)	.49 x .55 (.27)
Cost (.02)	.01 x .02 (0)	.22 x .02 (0)	.12 x .02 (0)
Total	.09	.21	**.37**

Then the team brainstormed possible countermeasures for potential problems. Options of hiring a part-time teacher and inexperienced candidate are selected.

x = Difficult:
Part-time teacher, inexperienced candidate selected

Milestones

- The school board chairman presented a written proposal to the school board, plan approved (3/5).
- The school board added the salary expenses to the proposed budget, finance committee approved it. Monitoring plan created.
- Jim Rudolph replaces team member Sue Rossi (3/16).

130 Creating a Storyboard   © 2000 GOAL/QPC

Project Plan Area	Project Plan	Actual Results	Variance	Reason
Schedule				
Advertise opening	4/12	4/12	0	
Interview 6 people/ make offer	4/25	4/26 (4 exper. candidates)	1 day	Tight labor market
Modify curriculum	10/2	10/1	1 day	
Re-survey parents	6/3	6/5	2 days	Copier broke
Budget				
Advertising expenses	$2,500	$2,700	$200	Used Web to advertise
Survey expenses	$150	$150	0	

The new teacher was hired on schedule. The advertising and survey expenses were just above budget. Curriculum was modified on schedule.

Milestones
- Finance committee approved proposed budget with some debate (3/16).
- Offer accepted, new hire began at the start of the new school year with a one-year contract (6/14).
- Principal, team approved new curriculum (10/1).

Step 6. Review and Evaluate the Results of the Change

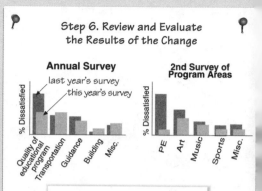

Annual Survey

% Dissatisfied

last year's survey
this year's survey

Quality of educational program, Transportation, Guidance, Building, Misc.

2nd Survey of Program Areas

% Dissatisfied

PE, Art, Music, Sports, Misc.

1. 65% of the annual surveys are returned, showing 25% improvement in satisfaction with overall quality.
2. 2nd survey of program areas shows 60% decrease in dissatisfaction with PE program.
3. Number of behavior problems reported to principal is reduced by 20%.
4. Number of excuses from nurse decreases 10%.

Milestones

- Team sent survey results and a letter to the school board recommending that the new teacher be retained permanently (10/4).
- Team presented survey results at a school board meeting (10/7).
- Team leader wrote parent newsletter article describing curriculum changes and the results of the survey (10/7).

Step 7. Reflect and Act on Learnings

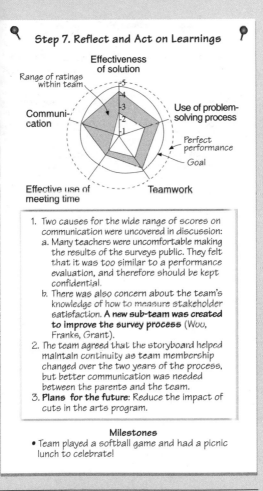

1. Two causes for the wide range of scores on communication were uncovered in discussion:
   a. Many teachers were uncomfortable making the results of the surveys public. They felt that it was too similar to a performance evaluation, and therefore should be kept confidential.
   b. There was also concern about the team's knowledge of how to measure stakeholder satisfaction. **A new sub-team was created to improve the survey process** (Woo, Franke, Grant).
2. The team agreed that the storyboard helped maintain continuity as team membership changed over the two years of the process, but better communication was needed between the parents and the team.
3. **Plans for the future:** Reduce the impact of cuts in the arts program.

Milestones
- Team played a softball game and had a picnic lunch to celebrate!

Storyboarding References

Forsha, Harry I. *Show Me: The Complete Guide to Storyboarding and Problem Solving.* Milwaukee, WI: ASQ Press, 1995.

Raymond, Larry. *Reinventing Communication: A Guide to Using Visual Language for Planning, Problem Solving, and Reengineering.* Milwaukee, WI: ASQ Press, 1994.

Ritter, Diane and Michael Brassard. *The Creativity Tools Memory Jogger™.* Salem, NH: GOAL/QPC, 1998, 165–167.

Tufte, Edward R. *Envisioning Information.* Cheshire, CT: Graphics Press, 1990.

Types of Measures

Measure	Description
Quality	Key product or service characteristics of interest to you and the customer: mistakes, failures, complaints, returned items, repairs, time, etc.
People	Information about the people doing the job that will impact performance or product: grade level, age, experience, skill, individual.
Equipment	Equipment used to produce product or service: computers, heavy equipment, presses, copiers, phones, buses, ovens, tools, instruments–by kind, manufacturer, lot, etc.
Material	Materials that go into the product or service: electronic components, paper, solvent, resin, paints, books, videos, pens–by kind, manufacturer, lot, etc.
Procedure	How things are done or carried out: what conditions, methods, orders, arrangement, etc.
Environment	Conditions around the process that might impact the quality of product or service: building, room, temperature.
Cost	Time, expenses, staffing.
Delivery	What may impact delivery of the product or service to your customer: instructions, shortages, defaults in payments, delays in delivery, wait time.

Continued on next page

Types of Measures, continued

Measure	Description
Safety	Accidents, mistakes, breakdowns.
Reliability	The ability to produce the services promised, dependably and accurately.
Responsiveness	The wilingness to help customers and provide prompt service.
Courtesy	Politeness, respect, consideration, and friendliness.
Competence	Having the skills and knowledge needed to perform the service customers desire.
Credibility	Being a service provider that is trustworthy, believable, and honest.
Accessibility	Ease of access and ease of contact.
Communication	Verbal interactions with the customers—keeping customers informed, using language they understand, and listening to them and their concerns.
Understanding	Finding out the needs, expectations, and satisfaction levels of the customers.
Tangibles	The physical facilities in which the service is provided, the equipment used in its delivery, the appearance of the service personnel, and the materials used to communicate.

Appendix
B

Advanced Techniques Resource List

This appendix contains brief descriptions and references to more advanced techniques for problem solving. In-depth descriptions of these methods are beyond the scope of this book. However, readers who want to refine their problem-solving skills can refer to the resources listed below.

Design of Experiments

A statistical process for determining the effects of changes that are introduced into a process under controlled conditions. The purpose of the experimentation is to make a process more robust by reducing possible sources of variation that could destabilize the process.

Taguchi, Genichi and Yoshiko Yokoyama. *Taguchi Methods: Design of Experiments*. Quality Engineering, Volume 4. Novi, MI: American Supplier Institute, 1993.

Barrentine, Larry B. *An Introduction to Design of Experiments: A Simplified Approach*. Milwaukee, WI: ASQ Press, 1999.

Failure Mode and Effect Analysis

An analytical process, usually conducted during product development, in which potential product defects and problems with use are identified and evaluated for severity. Once failure modes have been identified, design modifications are made to eliminate these sources of failure.

Stamatis, D. H. *Failure Mode and Effect Analysis: FMEA from Theory to Execution.* Milwaukee, WI: ASQ Press, 1995.

McDermott, Robin E., Raymond J. Mikulak, and Michael R. Beauregard. *The Basics of FMEA.* New York, NY: Quality Resources, 1996.

Is/Is Not Analysis

An analytical technique for identifying and validating the root cause of a problem. The analysis involves the identification of distinctive features in the problem condition (where it "is") that do not appear where the problem condition does not exist (where it "is not"). These distinctions are possible causes of the problem and are subjected to further testing to verify the true root cause of the problem.

Kepner, Charles, and Benjamin Tregoe. *The New Rational Manager.* Princeton, NJ: Princeton Research Press, 1981. (See Chapter 2.)

Six Sigma Quality

Six sigma quality is both a philosophy and a methodology in which an organization continuously improves its processes until they are virtually defect-free. Six sigma is a statistically derived measure of a process that consistently produces no more than 3.4 defects (or failures) for every one million outputs. The higher the sigma level, the lower the defect rate, e.g., a "one sigma process" produces 32% defects, a "two sigma process," 5% defects, a "three sigma process" 0.3%, and a "six sigma process" is 99.9997% defect-free.

Harry, Mikel J. *The Nature of Six Sigma Quality.* Schaumburg, IL: Motorola University Press, 1997.

Breyfogle, Forrest W. *Implementing Six Sigma: Smarter Solutions Using Statistical Methods.* New York, NY: John Wiley & Sons, Inc., 1999.

TRIZ

TRIZ, which in Russian stands for "Theory of Inventive Problem Solving," is a systematic approach for creating innovative solutions to technical problems. It is especially useful for new product development, service delivery, and solving production problems.

Genrich S. Altshuller and others devoted more than 50 years of research into understanding how inventive or breakthrough solutions were found. This research defined 11 conceptual elements that have been used to solve problems and produce patentable solutions.

Altshuller, Genrich S. *40 Principles: TRIZ Keys to Technical Innovation.* Worcester, MA: Technical Innovation Center, Inc., 1997.

Altshuller, Genrich S. *The Innovation Algorithm: TRIZ Systematic Innovation and Technical Creativity.* Worcester, MA: Technical Innovation Center, Inc., 1999.

GOAL/QPC Research Committee. *TRIZ Research Report: An Approach to Systematic Innovation.* Salem, NH: GOAL/QPC, 1997.

A p p e n d i x
C

Control Charts—Recognizing Sources of Variation

This appendix describes how to construct and interpret several types of Control Charts. The information is reproduced from *The Memory Jogger™ II*, pp. 36–51.

For additional information on Control Charts, consult the *Coach's Guide to The Memory Jogger™ II*, pp. 45–62 or the Control Chart guides available as part of *The Memory Jogger™ II Off-the-Shelf Modular Training Materials*.

Control Charts

Recognizing sources of variation

Why use it?

To monitor, control, and improve process performance over time by studying variation and its source.

What does it do?

- Focuses attention on detecting and monitoring process variation over time
- Distinguishes special from common causes of variation, as a guide to local or management action
- Serves as a tool for ongoing control of a process
- Helps improve a process to perform consistently and predictably for higher quality, lower cost, and higher effective capacity
- Provides a common language for discussing process performance

How do I do it?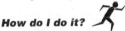

There are many types of Control Charts. The Control Chart(s) that your team decides to use will be determined by the type of data you have. Use the Tree Diagram on the next page to determine which Control Chart(s) will best fit your situation. Other types of Control Charts, which are beyond the scope of this book, include the Pre-Control Chart, the Moving Average & Range Chart, the Cumulative Sum Chart, and Box Plots.

Based on the type of data and sample size you have, choose the appropriate Control Chart.

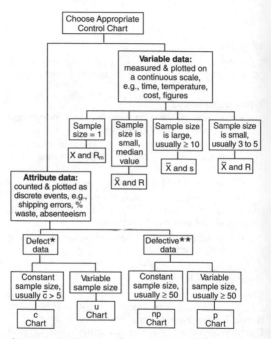

* Defect = Failure to meet one of the acceptance criteria. A defective unit might have multiple defects.

** Defective = An entire unit fails to meet acceptance criteria, regardless of the number of defects on the unit.

Constructing Control Charts

1. **Select the process to be charted.**

2. **Determine sampling method and plan.**
   - How large a sample can be drawn? Balance the time and cost to collect a sample with the amount of information you will gather. *See the Tree Diagram on the previous page for suggested sample sizes.*
   - As much as possible, obtain the samples under the same technical conditions: the same machine, operator, lot, and so on.
   - Frequency of sampling will depend on whether you are able to discern patterns in the data. Consider hourly, daily, shifts, monthly, annually, lots, and so on. Once the process is "in control," you might consider reducing the frequency with which you sample.
   - Generally, collect 20–25 groups of samples before calculating the statistics and control limits.
   - Consider using historical data to set a baseline.

   Tip Make sure samples are random. To establish the inherent variation of a process, allow the process to run untouched, i.e., according to standard procedures.

3. **Initiate data collection.**
   - Run the process untouched, and gather sampled data.
   - Record data on an appropriate Control Chart sheet or other graph paper. Include any unusual events that occur.

---

4. Calculate the appropriate statistics.

a) If you have attribute data, use the Attribute Data Table, Central Line column.

Attribute Data Table

Type Control Chart	Sample size	Central Line	Control Limits
Fraction defective p Chart	Variable, usually ≥50	For each subgroup: $p = np/n$ For all subgroups: $\bar{p} = \Sigma np/\Sigma n$	$*UCL_p = \bar{p} + 3\sqrt{\dfrac{\bar{p}(1-\bar{p})}{n}}$ $*LCL_p = \bar{p} - 3\sqrt{\dfrac{\bar{p}(1-\bar{p})}{n}}$
Number defective np Chart	Constant, usually ≥50	For each subgroup: $np = $ # defective units For all subgroups: $n\bar{p} = \Sigma np/k$	$UCL_{np} = n\bar{p} + 3\sqrt{n\bar{p}(1-\bar{p})}$ $LCL_{np} = n\bar{p} - 3\sqrt{n\bar{p}(1-\bar{p})}$
Number of defects c Chart	Constant	For each subgroup: $c = $ # defects For all subgroups: $\bar{c} = \Sigma c/k$	$UCL_c = \bar{c} + 3\sqrt{\bar{c}}$ $LCL_c = \bar{c} - 3\sqrt{\bar{c}}$
Number of defects per unit u Chart	Variable	For each subgroup: $u = c/n$ For all subgroups: $\bar{u} = \Sigma c/\Sigma n$	$*UCL_u = \bar{u} + 3\sqrt{\dfrac{\bar{u}}{n}}$ $*LCL_u = \bar{u} - 3\sqrt{\dfrac{\bar{u}}{n}}$

$np = $ # defective units
$c = $ # of defects
$n = $ sample size within each subgroup
$k = $ # of subgroups

* This formula creates changing control limits. To avoid this, use average sample sizes $\bar{n}$ for those samples that are within ±20% of the average sample size. Calculate individual limits for the samples exceeding ±20%.

b) If you have variable data, use the Variable Data Table, Central Line column.

Variable Data Table

Type Control Chart	Sample size n	Central Line*	Control Limits
Average & Range	<10, but usually 3 to 5	$\bar{\bar{X}} = \dfrac{(\bar{X}_1 + \bar{X}_2 + \ldots \bar{X}_k)}{k}$	$UCL_{\bar{x}} = \bar{\bar{X}} + A_2\bar{R}$ $LCL_{\bar{x}} = \bar{\bar{X}} - A_2\bar{R}$
$\bar{X}$ and R		$\bar{R} = \dfrac{(R_1 + R_2 + \ldots R_k)}{k}$	$UCL_R = D_4\bar{R}$ $LCL_R = D_3\bar{R}$
Average & Standard Deviation	Usually ≥10	$\bar{\bar{X}} = \dfrac{(\bar{X}_1 + \bar{X}_2 + \ldots \bar{X}_k)}{k}$	$UCL_{\bar{x}} = \bar{\bar{X}} + A_3\bar{s}$ $LCL_{\bar{x}} = \bar{\bar{X}} - A_3\bar{s}$
$\bar{X}$ and s		$\bar{s} = \dfrac{(s_1 + s_2 + \ldots s_k)}{k}$	$UCL_s = B_4\bar{s}$ $LCL_s = B_3\bar{s}$
Median & Range	<10, but usually 3 or 5	$\bar{\bar{X}} = \dfrac{(\tilde{X}_1 + \tilde{X}_2 + \ldots \tilde{X}_k)}{k}$	$UCL_{\bar{x}} = \bar{\bar{X}} + \tilde{A}_2\bar{R}$ $LCL_{\bar{x}} = \bar{\bar{X}} - \tilde{A}_2\bar{R}$
$\tilde{X}$ and R		$\bar{R} = \dfrac{(R_1 + R_2 + \ldots R_k)}{k}$	$UCL_R = D_4\bar{R}$ $LCL_R = D_3\bar{R}$
Individuals & Moving Range	1	$\bar{X} = \dfrac{(X_1 + X_2 + \ldots X_k)}{k}$	$UCL_X = \bar{X} + E_2\bar{R}_m$ $LCL_X = \bar{X} - E_2\bar{R}_m$
X and R_m		$R_m = |(X_{i+1} - X_i)|$ $\bar{R}_m = \dfrac{(R_1 + R_2 + \ldots R_{k-1})}{k-1}$	$UCL_{Rm} = D_4\bar{R}_m$ $LCL_{Rm} = D_3\bar{R}_m$

k = # of subgroups, $\tilde{X}$ = median value within each subgroup

*$\bar{X} = \dfrac{\sum X_i}{n}$

5. **Calculate the control limits.**
   a) If you have attribute data, use the Attribute Data Table, Control Limits column.
   b) If you have variable data, use the Variable Data Table, Control Limits column for the correct formula to use.
   - Use the Table of Constants to match the numeric values to the constants in the formulas shown in the Control Limits column of the Variable Data Table. The values you will need to look up will depend on the type of Variable Control Chart you choose and on the size of the sample you have drawn.

   Tip If the Lower Control Limit (LCL) of an Attribute Data Control Chart is a negative number, set the LCL to zero.

   Tip The p and u formulas create changing control limits if the sample sizes vary subgroup to subgroup. To avoid this, use the average sample size, n, for those samples that are within ±20% of the average sample size. Calculate individual limits for the samples exceeding ±20%.

6. **Construct the Control Chart(s).**
   - For Attribute Data Control Charts, construct one chart, plotting each subgroup's proportion or number defective, number of defects, or defects per unit.
   - For Variable Data Control Charts, construct two charts: on the top chart plot each subgroup's mean, median, or individuals, and on the bottom chart plot each subgroup's range or standard deviation.

Table of Constants

Sample size n	$\bar{X}$ and R Chart			$\bar{X}$ and s Chart			
	A_2	D_3	D_4	A_3	B_3	B_4	c_4*
2	1.880	0	3.267	2.659	0	3.267	.7979
3	1.023	0	2.574	1.954	0	2.568	.8862
4	0.729	0	2.282	1.628	0	2.266	.9213
5	0.577	0	2.114	1.427	0	2.089	.9400
6	0.483	0	2.004	1.287	0.030	1.970	.9515
7	0.419	0.076	1.924	1.182	0.118	1.882	.9594
8	0.373	0.136	1.864	1.099	0.185	1.815	.9650
9	0.337	0.184	1.816	1.032	0.239	1.761	.9693
10	0.308	0.223	1.777	0.975	0.284	1.716	.9727

Sample Size n	$\bar{X}$ and R Chart			X and R_m Chart			
	$\tilde{A}_2$	D_3	D_4	E_2	D_3	D_4	d_2*
2	----	0	3.267	2.659	0	3.267	1.128
3	1.187	0	2.574	1.772	0	2.574	1.693
4	----	0	2.282	1.457	0	2.282	2.059
5	0.691	0	2.114	1.290	0	2.114	2.326
6	----	0	2.004	1.184	0	2.004	2.534
7	0.509	0.076	1.924	1.109	0.076	1.924	2.704
8	----	0.136	1.864	1.054	0.136	1.864	2.847
9	0.412	0.184	1.816	1.010	0.184	1.816	2.970
10	----	0.223	1.777	0.975	0.223	1.777	3.078

* Useful in estimating the process standard deviation $\hat{\sigma}$.

Note: The minimum sample size in this chart is 2 because variation in the form of a range can only be calculated in samples greater than 1. The X and R_m Chart creates these minimum samples by combining and then calculating the difference between sequential, individual measurements.

- Draw a solid horizontal line on each chart. This line corresponds to the process average.
- Draw dashed lines for the upper and lower control limits.

Interpreting Control Charts

- **Attribute Data Control Charts** are based on one chart. The charts for fraction or number defective, number of defects, or number of defects per unit, measure variation *between samples*. **Variable Data Control Charts** are based on two charts: the one on top, for averages, medians, and individuals, measures variation *between subgroups* over time; the chart below, for ranges and standard deviations, measures variation *within subgroups* over time.

- Determine if the process mean (center line) is where it should be relative to your customer specifications or your internal business needs or objectives. If not, then it is an indication that something has changed in the process, or the customer requirements or objectives have changed.

- Analyze the data relative to the control limits; distinguishing between *common* causes and *special* causes. The fluctuation of the points within the limits results from variation inherent in the process. This variation results from common causes within the system, e.g., design, choice of machine, preventive maintenance, and can only be affected by changing that system. However, points outside of the limits or patterns within the limits, come from a special cause, e.g., human errors, unplanned events, freak occurrences, that is not part of the way the process normally operates, or is present because of an unlikely combination of process steps. Special causes must be eliminated before the Control Chart can be used as a monitoring tool. Once this is done, the process will be "in control" and samples can be taken at regular intervals to make sure that the process doesn't fundamentally change. See "Determining if Your Process is Out of Control."

- Your process is in "statistical control" if the process is not being affected by special causes, the influence of an individual or machine. All the points must fall within the control limits and they must be randomly dispersed about the average line for an in-control system.

Tip "Control" doesn't necessarily mean that the product or service will meet your needs. It only means that the process is *consistent*. Don't confuse control limits with specification limits—specification limits are related to customer requirements, not process variation.

Tip Any points outside the control limits, once identified with a cause (or causes), should be removed and the calculations and charts redone. Points within the control limits, but showing indications of trends, shifts, or instability, are also special causes.

Tip When a Control Chart has been initiated and all special causes removed, continue to plot new data on a new chart, but DO NOT recalculate the control limits. As long as the process does not change, the limits should not be changed. Control limits should be recalculated only when a permanent, desired change has occurred in the process, and only using data *after* the change occurred.

Tip Nothing will change just because you charted
it! You need to do something. Form a team to
investigate. See "Common Questions for Investi-
gating an Out-of-Control Process."

Determining if Your Process is "Out of Control"

A process is said to be "out of control" if either one of
these is true:

1. **One or more points fall outside of the control
limits**

2. **When the Control Chart is divided into zones, as
shown below, any of the following points are true:**

a) Two points, out of three consecutive points, are
on the same side of the average in Zone A or
beyond.

b) Four points, out of five consecutive points, are on
the same side of the average in Zone B or beyond.

c) Nine consecutive points are on one side of the
average.

d) There are six consecutive points, increasing or
decreasing.

e) There are fourteen consecutive points that alter-
nate up and down.

f) There are fifteen consecutive points within Zone
C (above and below the average).

Tests for Control

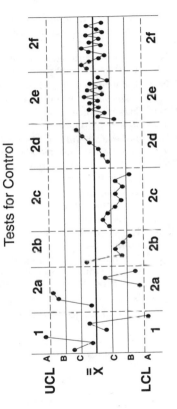

Source: Lloyd S. Nelson, Director of Statistical Methods, Nashua Corporation, New Hampshire

Common Questions for Investigating an Out-of-Control Process

❑ Yes ❑ No	Are there differences in the measurement accuracy of instruments/methods used?
❑ Yes ❑ No	Are there differences in the methods used by different personnel?
❑ Yes ❑ No	Is the process affected by the environment, e.g., temperature, humidity?
❑ Yes ❑ No	Has there been a significant change in the environment?
❑ Yes ❑ No	Is the process affected by predictable conditions? Example: tool wear.
❑ Yes ❑ No	Were any untrained personnel involved in the process at the time?
❑ Yes ❑ No	Has there been a change in the source for input to the process? Example: raw materials, information.
❑ Yes ❑ No	Is the process affected by employee fatigue?
❑ Yes ❑ No	Has there been a change in policies or procedures? Example: maintenance procedures.
❑ Yes ❑ No	Is the process adjusted frequently?
❑ Yes ❑ No	Did the samples come from different parts of the process? Shifts? Individuals?
❑ Yes ❑ No	Are employees afraid to report "bad news"?

A team should address each "Yes" answer as a potential source of a special cause.

Individuals & Moving Range Chart
IV Lines Connection Time

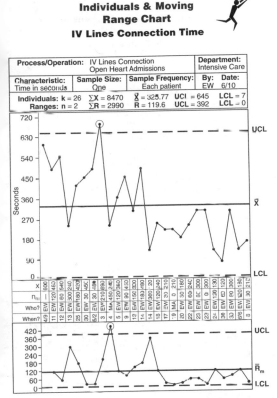

Process/Operation:	IV Lines Connection Open Heart Admissions		Department: Intensive Care	
Characteristic: Time in seconds	Sample Size: One	Sample Frequency: Each patient	By: EW	Date: 6/10
Individuals: k = 26 ∑X = 8470 X̄ = 325.77 UCL = 645 LCL = 7				
Ranges: n = 2 ∑R = 2990 R̄ = 119.6 UCL = 392 LCL = 0				

Information provided courtesy of Parkview Episcopal Medical Center

Note: Something in the process changed, and now it takes less time to make IV connections for patients being admitted for open heart surgery.

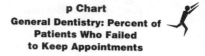

p Chart
General Dentistry: Percent of Patients Who Failed to Keep Appointments

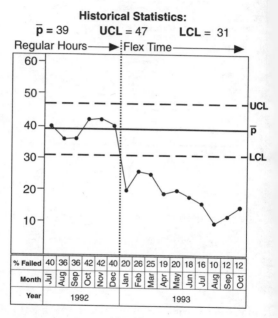

Historical Statistics:

$\bar{p} = 39$ UCL = 47   LCL = 31

Regular Hours ──────► Flex Time ──────────►

% Failed	40	36	36	42	42	40	20	26	25	19	20	18	16	10	12	12
Month	Jul	Aug	Sep	Oct	Nov	Dec	Jan	Feb	Mar	Apr	May	Jun	Jul	Aug	Sep	Oct
Year	1992						1993									

Information provided courtesy of U.S. Navy, Naval Dental Center, San Diego

Note: Providing flex time for patients resulted in fewer appointments missed.

u Chart
Shop Process Check
Solder Defects

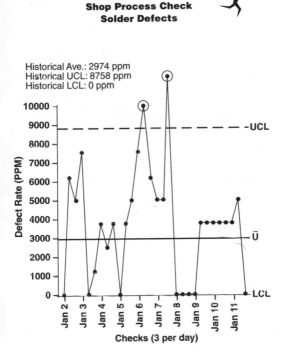

Historical Ave.: 2974 ppm
Historical UCL: 8758 ppm
Historical LCL: 0 ppm

Information provided courtesy of AT&T

X̄ & R Chart
Overall Course Evaluations

n = 10 evaluations randomly sampled each week
1-Not at all   2-Not very   3-Moderately   4-Very   5-Extremely

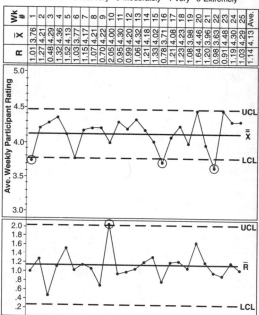

Wk #	1	2	3	4	5	6	7	8	9	10	11	12	13	14	15	16	17	18	19	20	21	22	23	24	25	Ave.
X̄	3.76	4.21	4.29	4.36	4.13	3.77	4.17	4.21	4.22	4.00	4.30	4.20	4.32	4.18	4.02	3.71	4.08	3.98	4.23	4.46	3.96	3.63	4.48	4.30	4.29	4.13
R	1.01	1.27	0.48	1.32	1.52	1.03	1.15	1.07	0.70	2.05	0.95	0.99	1.06	1.21	1.33	0.78	1.23	1.08	1.64	1.20	0.98	0.91	1.19	1.03	1.03	1.14

Information provided courtesy of Hamilton Standard

Note: Weeks 1, 10 (from bottom chart), 16, and 22 should be reviewed to understand why the ratings are outside the control limits.

ndex

action plan, 63, 75–79
activity network diagram, 86–88
attribute data, 21, 144
  use in Pareto Charts, 24
cause and effect diagram, 46–50
  examples, 52, 56
  selecting cause categories, 47
cause and effect relationships,
  45–46
common causes, 45, 148
control charts, 140–156
  definition, 13, 141
  examples, 153–156
  interpretation, 148–152
control limits, 146
countermeasures, 63, 79
customer
  definition, 2
  and supplier relationships, 36
data
  how to use in problem solving,
  21, 23, 54
  types, 21
  See also attribute data, variable
  data
Deming cycle, 11
design of experiments, 137
documentation of a process,
  36–44
failure mode and effect analysis
  (FMEA), 137–138
flowchart
  deployment flowchart, 44
  examples, 39, 43, 44, 110
  how to create, 37–38
  top-down flowchart, 43
  validation, 40–43
Gantt chart, 78, 84

input measures, 6
interrelationship digraph, 60–61
is/is not analysis, 138
leadership, 9, 92
learning organization, 114
matrix diagram, 58–59, 67, 78, 83
measures
  types of, 6–7
morphological box, 89–91
outcome measures, 6–7
Pareto principle, 24
Pareto chart examples, 31, 32
PDCA Cycle
  as a systematic approach,
  11–13
  definition, 12
  purpose, 11
performance gap
  how to improve it, 3–4
prioritization matrices example,
  68–73
problem
  definition, 3
  identification, 20–35
  statement, 33
problem reformulation tool, 34
problems and causes
  See cause and effect diagram,
  cause and effect relationships,
  root causes, variation
problem solving
  definition, 3
  key success factors, 7–10
  overview, 1–10
  taking a systematic approach, 4
  team assessment of process,
  115–118
  See also PDCA cycle

process
    definition, 2
    how to describe, 37–44
    out of control, 150–152
    variation, 13
process decision program chart
    (PDPC), 79, 85
process documentation, 37,
    106–107
process improvement
    and motivation and morale, 93
    and standardization, 105–113
    evaluating results, 102–104
    how to present results, 108–109
    definition, 5
    See also storyboards
process performance
    how to measure, 21, 23–24
process performance measures,
    6–7, 22
    definition, 5
    examples, 25, 135–136
    See also attribute data, variable
    data
process standardization, 105–113
purpose hierarchy, 35
responsibility matrix, 78, 83
root cause identification, 46, 55,
    58–61
root cause analysis, 46
run chart examples, 27
seven-step model
    features, 15
    implementation of steps,
    19–120
    purpose, 14
    snapshot, vi
    steps, tasks, and tools table,
    16–18

six sigma quality, 138–139
solutions
    criteria for selecting, 66
    implementing, 73, 75–79,
    92–100
    ranking solutions with tools,
    66–73
solution statement, 64–65
special causes, 46, 148
statistical control, 149
storyboards, 99, 121–134
    content and display, 123–125
    example, 126–134
    materials needed, 122
    purpose, 121
supplier
    definition, 2
table of constants, 147
team membership, 7–8, 28
tree diagram, 77, 81–82, 142
TRIZ, 139
variable data, 21, 145
    use in run and control charts,
    23
variation, 13, 45–46
weighted criteria decision matrix,
    58–59
work
    defined as a process, 2

Notes

Ordering Information: 5 Ways to Order

CALL TOLL FREE
1-800-643-4316
or 603-893-1944
8:30 AM – 5:00 PM EST

MAIL
GOAL/QPC
12B Manor Parkway
Salem, NH
03079-2862

WEB SITE
www.goalqpc.com

FAX
603-870-9122

E-MAIL
service@goalqpc.com

Price Per Copy

1–9	$10.95
10-24	15% discount
25–99	20% discount
100–499	30% discount

For quantities of 500 or more, call for a quote.

Sales Tax

Canada	7% of order
Massachusetts	5% of order

Shipping & Handling Charges

Continental US: Orders up to $10 = $2 (US Mail). Orders $10 or more = $4 + 4% of order (guaranteed Ground Delivery). Call for overnight, 2 & 3 day delivery. **For Alaska, Hawaii, Canada, Puerto Rico and other countries, please call.**

Payment Methods

We accept payment by check, money order, credit card, or purchase order. **If you pay by purchase order**: 1) Provide the name and address of the person to be billed, or 2) Send a copy of the P.O. when order is payable by an agency of the federal government.

Order Form for
The Problem Solving Memory Jogger™

1. Shipping Address (We cannot ship to a P.O. Box)

Name _____

Title _____

Company _____

Address _____

City _____

State _____ Zip _____ Country _____

Phone _____ Fax _____

E-mail _____

2. Quantity & Price

Code	Quantity	Unit Price	Total Price
1070E			
		Tax MA & Canada only	
		Shipping & Handling See opposite page	
		Total	

3. Payment Method

❑ Check enclosed (payable to GOAL/QPC) $ _____

❑ VISA ❑ MasterCard ❑ Amex ❑ Diners Club ❑ Discover

   Card # _____ Exp. date _____

   Signature _____

❑ Purchase order # _____

Bill to _____

Address _____

City _____

State _____ Zip _____ Country _____

4. Request for Other Materials

❑ Information on products, courses & training

❑ Information on customization

000X2

The Creativity Tools Memory Jogger™

This practical, low-cost guide supplies teams with the tools and techniques they need to develop their everyday, offbeat, creative ideas into innovative and unique solutions. This pocket guide can help everyone in your organization to generate new ideas when solving problems, developing new products, and improving processes. It includes guidelines on building a creative organizational environment, the use and benefits of 10 creativity tools, step-by-step examples and illustrations for all the tools, a start-to-finish case example for each tool, and several activities for exercising team creativity.

Code: 1055E

The Memory Jogger™ 9000/2000

Now you can understand and implement ISO 9001:2000 quickly, easily, and effectively. *The Memory Jogger™ 9000/2000* will guide you through the latest modifications to the ISO 9001 standard, with easy-to-follow instructions to prepare for, implement, and maintain ISO registration. This powerful pocket guide provides each employee with a clear understanding of the changes in terminology and clause structure from the 1994 standard, and answers key questions about each employee's role in the registration process. *The Memory Jogger™ 9000/2000* will be a cornerstone for the successful registration and implementation of ISO 9001:2000 in any organization. 2000. 180 pages. ISBN 1-57681-032-1. 3.5" x 5.5".

Code: 1065E

Facilitation at a Glance!

This pocket guide, written by Ingrid Bens and co-published by GOAL/QPC and AQP, describes facilitation behaviors and tools, the stages of facilitation, best and worst facilitator practices, how to facilitate conflict during meetings, effective decision making, techniques for getting everyone to participate, and much more. The many examples, checklists, and surveys can help anyone master the skills needed to facilitate meetings effectively.

Code: 1062E

The Team Memory Jogger™

Easy to read and written from the team member's point of view, *The Team Memory Jogger*™ goes beyond basic theories to provide you with practical nuts-and-bolts action steps on preparing to be an effective team member, how to get a good start, get work done in teams, and when and how to end a project. *The Team Memory Jogger*™ also teaches you how to deal with problems that can arise within a team. It's perfect for all employees at all levels.

Code: 1050E

The Memory Jogger™ II

This pocket guide is designed to help you improve the procedures, systems, quality, cost, and yields related to your job. *The Memory Jogger™ II* combines the basic Quality Tools and the Seven Management and Planning Tools in an easy-to-use format. It includes continuous improvement tools such as the Cause and Effect Diagram, Histogram, Run Chart, Pareto Chart, and many more!

Code: 1030E

Project Management Memory Jogger™

The *Project Management Memory Jogger™* is the most cost-effective way to ensure that your project teams achieve high-quality results. It provides every member of your organization with an easy-to-use roadmap for managing all types of projects. Whether your team is planning the construction of a new facility or implementing a customer feedback system, this pocket guide helps you avoid typical problems and pitfalls and create successful project outcomes every time. It is packed with useful information on everything from project concept to completion.

Code: 1035E

Customization of Your GOAL/QPC Books

Customize GOAL/QPC products with your company's name and logo, mission or vision statement, and almost anything else.

Benefits of customization
- Allows you more flexibility in determining content
- Gives your leaders an opportunity to personalize every copy
- Helps to promote your company's quality improvement efforts
- Communicates your organization's commitment to quality
- Helps lower the costs of in-house development of training materials
- Helps employees understand how they can help achieve company goals
- Gives your team a common vision

A few details
- Please allow a minimum of *4 weeks* for delivery of customized products.
- Customization is most cost effective for quantities of *200 or more*.
- Ask us about customizing GOAL/QPC products in other languages.

Call Toll Free: 800-643-4316
Phone: 603-893-1944 or Fax: 603-870-9122
E-mail: service@goalqpc.com
Web site: http://www.goalqpc.com